best *wine* buys

in the high street

2003

GW00634825

best **wine** buys
in the high street

2003

ned halley

foulsham
LONDON • NEW YORK • TORONTO • SYDNEY

foulsham

The Publishing House
Bennetts Close, Cippenham, Slough, Berkshire SL1 5AP, England

ISBN 0-572-02824-5

Printed in Great Britain by Cox & Wyman Ltd, Reading, Berkshire

Contents

A personal note

To keep the yearly editions of this book up to date, I go to a lot of wine tastings, especially those provided by the big supermarket chains. These occasions offer the chance to sniff and slurp from hundreds of bottles, and give a reasonably representative picture of the retailer's range – which can total anything up to a thousand different wines.

It sounds like a lot of diversity, but in the last year I have started to hear much more of the perennial complaint among my fellow sniffers, that far too many of the wines in supermarkets taste far too similar. There is continual carping that wines are made to a 'price point' rather than to any set of quality or character criteria.

Perhaps most surprisingly, given that over at least the last ten years we have enthusiastically endorsed the blue-sky merits of the 'New World' over the tradition-bound conservatism of Europe, the criticism seems to focus on the mass-produced wines of Australia, South Africa and both North and South America.

Australia, as we are repeatedly told of late, has now overtaken France as the principal supplier of wine to Britain – though in bulk terms rather than in value, it should be said. Actually I doubt if this is true, because one in six bottles of wine drunk here has been personally imported on 'booze cruises' from France and is thus probably French, and not entered into the Customs & Excise figures that have provided the figures showing Aussies on top.

But I digress. Australia, whatever the true figures, does supply a lot of the wine we drink in Britain. However, nearly all of it is accounted for by the giant brands – Jacob's Creek (owned, incidentally, by French multinational Pernod-Ricard), the massed brands of Hardy's, Lindemans and Penfolds – whose wines are genuinely ubiquitous. Very few supermarkets or high street off-licence chains dare not stock these wines. And the problem is, of course, that these big-name wines, not forgetting the similarly universal Gallo, Blossom Hill and Sutter Home brands from the USA, push smaller producers clean off the shelves.

It's an amazing achievement by the New World producers. Using just a handful of different imported French grape varieties grown in new, irrigated vineyards and employing cutting-edge technology, they have outsmarted European winemakers who have toiled for two thousand years to make wine everyone will like. Consider Portugal, which makes an astonishing variety of different wine styles and produces more wine than Australia: while a supermarket typically stocks more than 100 different wines from Australia alone, it is unlikely to have as many as 10 from Portugal.

In fairness to the retailers, many are well aware of the domination of brands, and it seems reasonable to assume that the fortunate people who buy in wines for the supermarkets or high street chains might feel a little threatened by them. After all, if stocking the shelves is simply a matter of re-ordering a few million more bottles of Jacob's Creek or Turning Leaf, why bother employing highly qualified Masters of Wine at enormous salaries to seek out more obscure wines?

Allan Cheesman, who has been buying wine for Sainsbury's for 30 years, and Tony Mason, who has done the same for Majestic for nearly as long, have both admitted to me that their emporiums are brimming with big brands. But both are adamant that they continue to source wine from out-of-the-way producers with whom they have dealt for many years, and continue to quest for interesting new discoveries. At the respective tastings of these two companies, I found sufficient numbers of such wines to justify a belief in what they said. Long may it last.

This year, as last, I have kept the ceiling on prices of recommended wines to £10, but as before the great majority of wines still come under the all-important £5 mark.

I have devoted most of the space here to the major national supermarket chains, because that's where we buy three-quarters of the wine we drink at home. Also here are the two outstanding 'high street' chains – Majestic and Oddbins.

Out this year is the chain known to itself as First Quench, but familiar to the rest of us as the sprawling chain of 2,500 off-licences variously called Thresher, Wine Rack, Bottoms Up and the moribund Victoria Wine. The object of perpetual mergers, take-overs and financial reorganisations, these shops have, in my opinion, entirely lost their way. I cannot find more than a handful of wines in any of their homogeneous branches worth recommending for interest or value.

Back in, on the other hand, is Marks & Spencer. Can it be coincidence that M&S's wines have revived in perfect synchrony with its clothes? Whatever the case, the range has expanded and improved almost out of recognition and Marks is now back at the top as far as wine value and quality are concerned.

As always, I must apologise in advance for the inevitable fact that some of the wines I have recommended will have been discontinued or replaced with a new vintage or increased (never decreased) in price by the time you read this. The year 2002 has seen a rise in the value of the euro against sterling of about 10 per cent, and this will no doubt be reflected in price increases for EU wines.

And I must reiterate that what I say about wines, and wine merchants, is based on my personal knowledge or understanding.

Taste is personal in all things, and more so than most when it comes to wine. But I hope the impressions I have given of the hundreds of wines recommended will tempt you to try some new styles, and to look beyond all those beckoning brand names to the genuine, individual wines still clinging to their shelf space.

The scoring system

As an entirely subjective guide to relative value among the wines mentioned in this book, I use a scoring scale of 0 to 12. In the notes I take while tasting, I give each wine a score within this range, and just about all the wines that score 8 or above are included.

As to those that score 7 or under, most are simply left out, because this is not a book in which there is space to decry wines I have not liked. So, the various (but not, thankfully, numerous) wines I have scored at 0 to 4 are all excluded. Those marked 5, 6 or 7 are not recommended as value for money, but are included for interest – either because they are decent wines that are overpriced or perhaps wines you might be tempted to buy because of their big brand name or gimmicky packaging, but which I found so disappointing I thought they merited a not-recommended warning.

Most of the wines featured in this edition score 8 or 9, which means they come recommended and I believe they are good value. If a wine scores 9/10 it's remarkably good value, and a straight 10 means I believe it is exceptionally delicious for the price. Anything marked 10/11 or above is quite simply a must-buy for anyone who enjoys the style of wine described.

For the record, this is approximately what each score in my system signifies to me, unless I make some contradictory comment in the individual note:

0   – undrinkable
1   – bad and expensive
2   – bad but cheap
3   – bad but cheap enough to cook with
4   – poor but just drinkable if cheap enough
5   – disappointing at the price
6   – decent but poor value
7   – good but a bit overpriced
8   – good and reasonably priced
9   – good and attractively priced
9/10 – very good and a bargain
10   – exceptionally good at the price
10/11 – outstanding, worth a special journey
11   – rare wine wildly underpriced
12   – none better (a score I have yet to award)

The choice

For each store mentioned in this book, the wines are categorised by nation of origin. This is largely to follow the manner in which retailers sort their wines, but also because it is the country or region of origin that still most distinguishes one style of wine from another. True, wines are now commonly labelled most prominently with their constituent grape variety, but to classify all the world's wines into the small number of principal grape varieties would make for categories of an unwieldy size.

Chardonnay and Sauvignon Blanc are overwhelmingly dominant among whites, and four grapes – Cabernet Sauvignon, Merlot, Shiraz and Tempranillo – account for a very high proportion of the red wines made worldwide.

But each area of production still – in spite of creeping globalisation – puts its own mark on its wines. Chardonnays from France remain (for the moment at least) quite distinct from those of Australia. Cabernet Sauvignon grown in a cool climate such as that of Bordeaux is a very different wine from Cabernet cultivated in the cauldron of the Barossa.

Of course there are 'styles' that winemakers worldwide seek to follow. Yellow, oaky Chardonnays of the type pioneered in South Australia are now made in South Africa, too – and in new, hi-tech wineries in New Zealand, Chile, Spain and Italy. But the variety is still wide. Even though the 'upfront' high-alcohol wines of the New World have grabbed so much of the market, France continues to produce the elegant wines it has always made in its classic regions; Germany still produces racy, delicate Rieslings; and the distinctive zones of Italy, Portugal and Spain make ever-more characterful wines from indigenous grapes (as opposed to imported global varieties).

Among less-expensive wines, the theme is, admittedly, very much a varietal one. The main selling point for most wines costing under £10 is the grape of origin rather than the country of origin. It makes sense, because the characteristics of various grape varieties do a great deal to identify taste. A bottle of white wine labelled Chardonnay can reasonably be counted on to deliver that distinctive peachy or pineappley smell and soft, unctuous apple flavours. A Sauvignon Blanc should evoke gooseberries, green fruit and grassy freshness. And so on.

As to the best sources of wines under a fiver or a tenner, it will take only a brief look through this book to reveal that some parts of the world appear to offer a far bigger choice of cheaper wines than others do. The classic regions of France – Alsace, Bordeaux, Burgundy – make relatively few appearances, simply because their 'fine wines' are almost entirely priced above £10.

The wines of the Rhône and the Midi, including the vins de pays ('country wines'), on the other hand, appear very regularly. So do the wines of southern Italy, the emerging reactivated regions of Portugal and Spain and fast-expanding Argentina. All are proving a growing source of excellent-value wines.

And for all the domination of Chardonnay and Cabernet, there are plenty more grape varieties making their presence felt. Argentina, for example, has revived the fortunes of several French and Italian varieties that had become near-extinct at home. And the grape that (in my view) can make the most exciting of white wines, the Riesling, is now doing great things in the southern hemisphere as well as at home in Germany.

The global varieties are, indeed, everywhere, but this book describes wines made from no fewer than 60 different grape varieties (listed in A Brief Vocabulary, pages 147–75) grown in every corner of the winemaking world. Let's hope this generous and growing choice is the shape of things to come.

Lingenfelder Riesling 2001 from the Rheinpfalz in Germany is in the modern, crisp style – £4.99 at Oddbins

The state of the market

In the summer of 2002, the major consumer-research company Mintel published a report on European drinking trends. One revelation that must have brought sunshine into the hearts of the British wine trade was that, for the first time in history, the UK has as many wine drinkers as France.

Well, almost. Sixty-four per cent of adults in Britain are now wine drinkers, compared to 65 per cent of the French. It is the near-culmination of a remarkable trend since the 1950s, when barely 20 per cent of Britons professed to drink any kind of wine. True, we are still 'light' consumers of wine – drinking less than half the 70-or-so bottles a year the average French adult gets through – but our thirst for, and interest in, wine is the fastest growing of any significant market in the world.

In 1980, the average adult British drinker got through 10 bottles of wine (three-quarters of it white) a year. Now we drink 30 bottles a year – equally divided between white and red. I believe this is an extremely good thing. Wine, especially red wine, is by far the most beneficial of alcoholic drinks for health, and surely no other beverage brings as much pleasure. Brewers need to look to their laurels, because we now spend more on wine than we do on beer. And did you know there are fewer drinkers of Scotch whisky in Britain than there are in France?

Apart from wishing the whisky industry all success in every market, and regretting that virtually all the wine we drink in Britain is imported, this new trend in our drinking habits is surely to be commended.

And from the patriotic standpoint, don't worry too much about the import angle. British-based multinational companies have been moving into the worldwide wine business in a big way of late. In 2002, for example, Bristol-based giant Allied Domecq bought New Zealand's biggest wine company, Montana, and two of the most celebrated champagne producers, Mumm and Perrier Jouët. If wine-producers have to be owned by global corporations at all, they might as well be owned by British global corporations.

And just as production continues to be concentrated into the ownership of fewer and larger businesses, so does merchandising. I believe supermarkets will eliminate the traditional off-licence chains, and fear for individual, independent wine merchants – though those offering unique and specialised ranges of good wine will surely continue to prosper as the 'connoisseur' sector of the expanding overall market gently grows.

I am quite certain, whatever happens, that Britain will continued to be, as it has always been, the best country in the world in which to buy wine. Not the cheapest, thanks to a long Puritan tradition of trying to repress alcohol consumption through usurious taxes, but with by far the biggest choice and with easily the most knowledgeable wine trade worldwide.

Long may that trade continue to prosper.

Multiple monopoly

In a nation with so many traditional wine merchants, from grand London purveyors with Royal Warrants to tiny specialist firms importing the wines of just one region of France, it comes as a shock to find that three-quarters of all the wine bought 'off-licence' (for drinking at home) in Britain comes from supermarkets.

But are supermarkets selling quantity at the expense of quality? Not a bit of it. These huge companies take quality very seriously – among the bargain wines (nine out of every ten bottles sold in supermarkets cost under £5) as well as the 'fine' wines.

Tasting hundreds of supermarket wines every year as I do, I can honestly report finding few I could fairly describe as badly made or unpleasant to drink. But even making allowances for the jading effects of tasting dozens of wines at one session, I must confess to one slightly troubling discovery: the striking homogeneity of an awful lot of wines. Far too many taste the same as each other.

Fair's fair, there is in some cases a simple explanation for this – because many supermarket 'own-brand' wines *are* the same as each other. Big producers in every part of the world happily apportion their harvests between two, three or more British supermarket chains, bottling the new wine in one giant operation with pauses merely for changing the labels.

And why not? The more outlets there are for the excellent wines of Argentina or Australia, the better. But the sameness problem isn't really about the enviable success of New World exporters. It's more about the uniformity of style. Supermarkets have convinced themselves that they know what their customers want. Most of the wines on the shelves conform not only to the prices dictated by the wine buyers, but also to the styles they expect. Safeway, Sainsbury's and Tesco all have a hand in making many of the wines they sell, demanding that the products of wineries in every part of the world stick to the styles customers are perceived to demand.

At Marks & Spencer, all the 350 wines it sells in its astonishingly expanded and improved range have been made specifically for the company. It has a team of wine buyers who spend a third of their working life not just finding the wines, but standing over the winemakers telling them how they want their wines made.

Who but a really gigantic retailer can wield this kind of power among the world's winemakers? I suppose it doesn't matter as long as the small-scale producers who make wine according to their own preferences can find sympathetic retailers who will take them as they find them. That said, good luck to the supermarkets – who do offer a terrific choice, and certainly plenty of commendable wines under a fiver or tenner. Thus, the very extensive sections devoted to the major supermarkets in this book.

High-street low

Britain's high-street off-licence chains don't inspire confidence. The vast First Quench chain is set to shrink to something like 2,000 outlets from the nearly 3,000 of just a few years ago. And the next-biggest chain, Unwins, which is concentrated in London and the south of England, has announced reduced profits, and redundancies, in the last year.

It's a sign of the times, because off-licences simply aren't cool any more. Wine in particular has become just another grocery item, and specialist retailers in this sector look destined to go the same way as their counterparts in bakery, butchery and fishmongery – by becoming just another aisle or counter in a gigantic hypermarket.

Now that we tend to buy our wine a few bottles at a time, the supermarket has become even more the obvious choice of place to shop. Parking is the killer advantage enjoyed by supermarkets in this context. How many high street off-licences can offer you anywhere to put your car other than on the double yellow lines outside the shop?

Facing this kind of competition, one might expect the really big high-street chains to be revolutionising the way in which they trade. But I see no sign of it from any of them.

The price of wine

How do retailers price their wines? Some bottles seem inexplicably cheap, others unjustifiably expensive. But there is often a simple explanation. Big retailers work to price points. In wine, these are £2.99, £3.49, £3.99, even £9.99. You'll find very few bottles priced anywhere between these 50p spacings. A wine that wouldn't be profitable at £4.99 but would be at, say, £5.11, is priced at £5.49 in the hope that shoppers won't be wise to the fact that it is relatively poor value.

It's true that there are some wines on supermarket shelves priced at £3.29, £3.79 etc. But these price points occur with suspicious irregularity, and suggest that an awful lot of wines are being pushed the greater distance towards the next 49 and 99 pence points.

Price can be a poor guide to quality even at the best of times. The only means by which any of us can determine a wine's value is on personal taste. The ideal bottle is one you like very much and would buy again at the same price without demur.

But, just for curiosity's sake, it's fun to know what the wine itself actually costs, and what the retailer is making on it. This is how the costs break down for a French wine costing £4.49 in a supermarket. This is a slightly unusual purchase by a supermarket, because the wine is being bought direct from the vineyard where it was made. Usually, retail multiples buy their wines by a less-strenuous method, from agents and distributors in the UK.

Price paid by supermarket to supplier in France for the bottled wine	£1.40
Transport and insurance to UK	£0.28
Excise duty	£1.16
Cost to supermarket	£2.84
Supermarket's routine mark-up at 30%	£0.85
VAT at 17.5% on marked-up price	£0.65
Provisional shelf price	£4.34
Adjustment in price/VAT to price point	£0.15
Shelf price in supermarket	£4.49

The largest share of the money appears to go to the producer in France. But from his £1.40 he must pay the cost of growing and harvesting the grapes, pressing them, fermenting the juice, clarifying and treating the wine. Then he must bottle, cork, encapsulate, label and pack the wine into cartons. If his margin after these direct costs is 50p, he's doing well.

The prime profiteer, however, is not the supermarket, even though it makes a healthy £1 in mark-up. It is the Chancellor who does best, by miles. Excise duty and VAT are two of the cheapest taxes to collect and from this single bottle of wine, the Treasury pockets a princely £1.84.

Travellers to wine-producing countries are always thrilled to find that by taking their own bottles, jugs or plastic casks to rustic vineyards offering wine on tap they can buy drinkable stuff for as little as 50 pence a litre. What too few travellers appreciate is that, for the wine itself, that's about what the supermarkets are paying for it. When enjoying your bargain bottle of wine, it is interesting to reflect on the economic reality known as 'added value' – which dictates that the worthiest person in the chain, the producer, has probably earned less than 10 per cent of the final price.

Devereux wines from the Aude Vin de Pays region of southern France are keenly priced for their quality – £2.99 at Sainsbury's

Wine on the web

It's been another terrible year for e-commerce. Of the dozens of dedicated online wine companies inaugurated just three or four years ago, only a handful remain.

There are some big dotcom wine companies now trading, notably the Virgin enterprise and the amazing everywine.co.uk, sponsored by northern supermarket company Booths and, on last inspection of the site, claiming to have 22,235 different wines available. And chateauonline is still to be found on the net, offering a mere 3,000 different wines for delivery to most European nations.

Then there's Bordeaux Direct, also known as Laithwaites (after founder Tony Laithwaite), which claims to be Britain's biggest mail order wine firm and has a net presence as well as taking up yards of space in the Sunday colour supplements.

But for smaller fry and those without some brick to substantiate their click, I really do worry for the future of even the best-capitalised of e-tailers.

It has, however, been another steady year of progress for existing wine merchants who are doing a bit of dotcom on the side. The Queen's wine merchant, Berry Bros (founded 300 years ago), has proved an unlikely leader in the market. At the other end of the scale, waitrose.com reports steady business, Tesco is active online and Sainsbury's is still in partnership with Oddbins to sell wine via the web (as well as through direct mail and press advertising) through a joint venture called the Destination Wine Company.

But I really cannot see any substantial advantages to buying wine online. I can see the point of buying wine by mail order (whether you place your order by post, phone, fax or via the web seems to make little difference) from a specialist who has just one premises but with a unique range of wine, but I remain mystified why anyone would buy the usual brands – as sold by everyone from Asda to Oddbins – by any means other than popping into the nearest branch of any one of the fifty local retailers that sell it.

I rather suspect that some dotcom wine companies have hoped to make their fortunes by buying their wines only after they have sold them, so to speak. Because they don't have to display stock in the shop, they needn't go to the trouble and expense of paying the supplier for it, handing over the duty and VAT to Customs, and financing storage. In the virtual shop of the web, they can accept a customer's order (and perhaps the customer's money, too) before requesting the goods from their supplier (in a hell of a rush, presumably) and paying the requisite duty and tax. But this leaves no scope for next-day or even next-week delivery for the customer – which rather undermines the claimed immediacy of e-commerce.

Choice is another issue. Most dedicated e-tailers have very short lists of wine, bulked out by mixed-case offers or 'bin-end sales'. It seems that it is not yet practical to display, price and annotate more than a few dozen wines on a website. But for high-street merchants and supermarkets it's another story. The chains have head-office lists of as many as 700 different wines, but can't hope to offer the whole lot in any but their very biggest outlets. On the web, however, it's no problem. A favourite wine you can find in a Co-op superstore but not in a dinky Co-op convenience shop will probably be found on the Co-op website. The price will be the same as it is in the superstore, and delivery will be dependable – and free for orders worth a reasonable minimum.

How can the new e-tailers possibly compete? They have no shop window other than the web. It is not possible to buy a single bottle of wine to taste before deciding whether to go for a case or two. How can a web-only trader provide 'customer service'? A duff bottle bought from a supermarket (on the web or not) can be returned to any branch for a replacement and/or refund (yes, some supermarkets give both), but how do you return bad wine to cyberspace? There will always be lingering doubts about reliability. Will wines have been stored correctly; will delivery be guaranteed; will credit card payment to an unfamiliar e-tailer be secure?

At this stage, I cannot safely recommend shopping anywhere on the web for wine other than from the sites of well-established retailers, whether supermarkets, high-street operators like Majestic (an award-winning website), or specialised independent merchants. For these retailers, of course, internet trading is little more than an extension of their existing home-delivery operations. The only difference is that their lists can be viewed on screen instead of on paper, and orders can be placed by the same credit card over the net rather than over the phone, fax or – perish the thought – in an envelope with a stamp on it.

Cross-Channel shopping

Choosing wine at French prices is a lot more fun than trying to decipher the average wine website, but is it really worth travelling across the Channel for the sole purpose of stocking up for a few pounds less than you would pay at home? The short answer is yes. It's fun to visit France (or even, at a pinch, Belgium) and out of season it can be very cheap. High-speed ferries, catamarans and hovercrafts can carry you to historic Channel ports in an hour or two for just a few pounds if you take advantage of the perpetual ticket promotions in the national press. Discounted tickets through the Eurotunnel are never quite as cheap, but for train enthusiasts the journey is a treat in itself.

True, there is no longer any 'duty-free' shopping on board the ferries (there never was on the trains). But, as passengers on P&O Stena, SeaFrance and Hoverspeed have been discovering since the abolition of the old tax-perk, this has made no difference. You can still buy wine, spirits and other goodies on board the ships at prices that seem remarkably similar to those of the good old days of duty-free.

The reason for this curious continuity is that shipping companies are now buying their supplies duty-paid on the other side of the Channel – which in some cases is almost as cheap as buying those supplies on a 'duty-free' basis used to be. After all, the duty on wine in France is only 2p a 75cl bottle. In Spain, Italy and elsewhere in southern Europe, there's no duty on wine at all. VAT in France, at 20.6 per cent, is appreciably higher than the prevailing rate of 17.5 per cent here, but the ferry operators are absorbing the cost.

In effect, the ships are in direct competition with the supermarkets and hideous British-owned 'wine warehouses' in the Channel ports. But ferry operators cannot hope, really, to compete with France's huge and powerful hypermarket companies. Auchan, Cora, Continent, Leclerc and other retail multiples have enormous buying power and of course very much larger premises in which to display their goods. And the car park of a major out-of-town *hypermarché* has rather more room in which to manoeuvre a groaning trolley than does the vehicle deck of a roll-on-roll-off ferry.

As explained on page 24, wine prices are dramatically lower in French supermarkets than they are in their British counterparts. But there is a dramatic gap, too, between prices in British supermarkets and other retailers either side of the water.

You can discover this by visiting Tesco's 'Vin Plus' branch in the immense Cité Europe shopping centre at the Pas de Calais (near the Eurotunnel terminal) or Sainsbury's drinks shop next to Calais' Auchan megamarket. Oddbins also has a shop in Cité Europe, and this year Majestic has taken over the former Wine and Beer Company, with branches in Calais, Cherbourg and Le Havre.

To give a comparison of prices either side of the Channel, I have extracted a few examples from the respective French and British price lists of the newly internationalised Majestic network. The differences are interesting. Remember, the gap in excise duty between the two countries is £1.14 per bottle (£1.16 in the UK, 2p in France), but French VAT is higher, at 20.6p per £1-worth of wine, compared to 17.5p per £1-worth in Britain. So, if duty and VAT were the only differentials, a bottle of wine valued at £2 including mark-up by a French retailer would sell for £2.44, and for £3.71 in a British shop – a price difference of about 50 per cent. But as cross-Channel figures always demonstrate, the differentials are far more variable.

Wine	UK	France	Saving
De Telmont champagne	£13.99	£8.49	£5.50
Taittinger champagne	£24.99	£13.29	£11.70
Cuvée de Richard	£2.89	£1.29	£1.60
Cuvée des Amandiers	£2.99	£1.49	£1.50
Merlot Sica Limouxins	£3.49	£1.99	£1.50
Domaine de Raissac Viognier	£4.99	£3.99	£1.00
Sancerre Vacheron 2000	£10.99	£8.99	£2.00
Le Fauve Merlot 2000	£3.99	£2.49	£1.50
Ch Guiot Costières de Nîmes	£4.99	£3.99	£1.00
Dragon Tempranillo 2000	£3.99	£1.99	£2.00
Senorio de Los Llanos Reserva 1994	£4.99	£3.49	£1.50
Torres Viña Sol 2001	£4.49	£2.99	£1.50
Blanco Reserva Murrieta 1997	£8.49	£5.99	£2.50
Montepulciano d'Abruzzo 2000	£3.99	£1.69	£2.30
Santa Cristina 2000	£5.99	£3.99	£2.00
Vistasur Cabernet Sauvignon 2000	£4.99	£2.99	£2.00
Jacob's Creek Chardonnay 2000	£4.99	£2.79	£2.20
Lindemans Bin 65 Chardonnay 2001	£5.99	£4.49	£1.50
Coldridge Estate Merlot 2001	£3.79	£1.99	£1.80
Koonunga Hill Cabernet-Shiraz 2000	£6.99	£4.99	£2.00

These differences are in many cases far in excess of anything accounted for by mere differences in tax. But British set-ups like Majestic are still nothing like as cheap as some of the local retailers in the Channel ports, where very drinkable vins de pays can start at as little as e1, or about 65 pence.

And the fact is that it is infinitely more exciting to shop in the French *hypermarchés* than it ever can be to take the cautious route into just another branch of your retailer at home. Just about everything in French supermarkets is cheaper – not just the wine, spirits and beers – and there is a choice of fresh and preserved foods, in the larger superstores, that puts our own stores to shame. English is widely spoken, and bi-lingual signs are commonplace in the stores. And if you're using an appropriate credit card, paying the bill is no more complicated than it is in a supermarket at home.

There is no limit to the quantity or value of goods you can bring back from any EU member country, provided it is not intended for resale in the UK. British Customs & Excise long ago published 'guidelines' as to what it considers reasonable limits on drinks that can be deemed to be for 'personal consumption'. You can thus import, no questions asked, 90 litres of wine, 20 of fortified wine, 10 of spirits and 110 of beer. That's about as much as a couple travelling together (and therefore able to import twice the above quantities) could cram into a family car without threatening the well-being of its suspension.

Savings on beer and spirits are, if anything, even more dramatic than they are on wine. French duty on beer is 5p a pint, compared to 33p here. This means a case of beer typically costing £12–£15 here can be had for under a fiver in Calais. It seems crazy. Similarly, a 70cl bottle of London gin or a Scotch whisky costing £11–£12 here is yours for £7–£8 in France, where the duty on spirits is half the £5.48 charged here and the mark-ups lower.

As if these differentials were not enough, the Channel ports also teem with good-value restaurants and hotels. Boulogne and Calais, Dieppe and Dunkirk bristle with venues where you can enjoy a e20–e25 (£13–£16) menu of a standard that would set you back several times as much at home. And there are respectable hotels where a clean room with bath or shower, plus croissants and excellent coffee for breakfast, can be had for the equivalent of £25 a night.

Why are wines so much cheaper in French shops?

The price gaps between the big stores either side of the Channel are, as illustrated above, by no means entirely accounted for by the difference between UK excise duty and VAT and French duty and VAT. So what's going on?

It's not that British supermarkets set higher margins than their continental counterparts. But when it comes to wine, the differential between the same wine on sale in the Asda at Coventry and the Auchan at Calais arises from how those respective supermarkets apply their margins.

It goes like this. In France, retailers typically mark up wines at 30 per cent. In the UK, as it happens, retailers also mark up by around 30 per cent. The difference is that shops in Britain add the mark-up not to what they've paid to the producer, but to the duty paid and delivered (DPD) price.

In the UK, every bottle of still wine, regardless of quality or price, comes with an excise duty and shipping cost of around £1.40. So a bottle of wine the retailer buys for £1 from the producer has a DPD price of £2.40. Marked up by 30 per cent for the retailer's margin, that becomes £3.12. Add VAT at 17.5 per cent and the actual retail price turns into £3.66.

In France, it's different. The typical duty and shipping cost in the price of a bottle of French wine is 12p. So the DPD price of the £1 bottle is £1.12. Marked up by 30 per cent it becomes £1.32. Add French VAT at 20.6 per cent and the actual retail price is £1.59. That's more than £2 less than the price of the same bottle of wine on our side of the Channel.

So, as well as paying the extra shipping cost plus the £1.14 differential between UK and French excise duty, you're paying a further 38p of retailer mark-up.

Closures

This seems an apposite topic with which to conclude this year's introduction. Closure is the term in the wine trade for the type of cork, stopper or screwcap employed to 'close' bottles. Once upon a time the choice was between cork and cork. But the quality of cork products, mainly supplied from the cork oak plantations of Spain or Portugal, has been under question in recent years. More and more wines closed with 'natural' corks have been found to be suffering from a dread ailment called trichloroanisole (TCA), which is characterised by a horrible taint in the flavour. TCA is caused by an infection known as methylised trichlorophenol and most commonly invades wine via poorly disinfected corks, though it's only fair to add that it can also get into the wine from infected barrels or cellar premises.

The wine industry is understandably tight-lipped about what has become an epidemic. The worry that any bottle of wine might be ruined by TCA is the sort of backdrop that could diminish wine sales altogether. But this isn't just a scare story: I have heard from members of the wine trade that in some tastings one in ten bottles has been spoiled by a bad 'natural' cork – either from TCA or of such poor quality that air or other kinds of infection have invaded the wine, causing it to oxidise or to become spoiled to the point we know as 'corky' or 'corked'.

The cork manufacturers are battling to improve quality, but many big wine producers and retailers have lost patience and turned to other forms of closure.

First on the scene was the polymer bung – a plastic, cork-shaped item driven into the neck of the bottle just like a natural cork, and designed to be extracted with a conventional corkscrew. My own experience of these things has been less than inspiring. They can be so hard that you have a devil of a job getting the point of the corkscrew in. Then, once you've got the thing out, they can be hellishly difficult to unwind from the corkscrew, because they have a smooth finish that is hard to grip with your hand, and the 'grain' in them seems resistant to the unwinding of the helix.

Worse, polymer bungs have a tendency to slide further down into the neck of the bottle as you insert the tip of the corkscrew. You end up driving the thing into the wine. Very messy. And these hard objects are subsequently very difficult to jam back into the neck of an unfinished bottle – they don't compress in the way natural corks do.

So, personally, I see very little future for these things – however hard the manufacturers try to make them interesting by producing them in wild colours, or even making them look like the real thing with arty 'graining'.

We are told that plastic stoppers are inert and that therefore the wine can be kept lying on its side for as long as you like and contact between wine and polymer will never cause any reaction that could spoil the wine. Maybe so, but surely not proven until someone tests the claim – and that will take decades of cellaring the same batches of wine divided up between natural cork and plastic cork closures.

In the meantime, the closure that looks most likely to fill the gap, so to speak, is the screwcap. This is the same item that has been keeping spirits safely sealed for as long as anyone can remember. And it has perfectly obvious advantages. For one, if a screwcap can keep a high-alcohol liquor in good nick and not be eaten into by what one might assume would be the corrosive effects of an ardent spirit, there seems no likelihood the gentler alcohol in a wine will present any challenge. For another, you don't need a corkscrew. And for another, if you don't finish the wine at a sitting, you just screw the top back on.

I believe the screwcap is the future – the long-term future – for all 'everyday' wines. And the big retailers are moving in this direction. Tesco, Britain's biggest wine retailer, has introduced its own screwcap wines – wittily called the 'Unwind' range. In the summer of 2002, the chain introduced 30 such wines priced between £3.99 and £8.99, and in 10 weeks sold more than 1.5 million bottles. Its in-store surveys found that '60 per cent of respondents thought that screwcaps are a good idea for wine and 65 per cent said they would buy a wine sealed with one'. The company is cock-a-hoop with the success of its experiment – which has included demanding special screwcap bottlings of major brands like Jacob's Creek, Lindemans and Penfolds from the producers – and will now lean on more and more winemakers to abandon the cork in favour of the screwcap.

Some producers aren't waiting to be told. In New Zealand, where at a big national wine fair 30 per cent of one major group of wines was found to have been ruined by defective natural corks, a number of important growers have got together to find an alternative, and to publicise their view that screwcaps and the finest wines are by no means mutually exclusive.

The New Zealand Screwcap Wine Seal Initiative, which involves growers such as Kim Crawford and Bob Campbell (both stars in the Kiwi wine firmament), makes these bold assertions:

- Screwcap wine seals do not introduce the risk of extraneous 'taint' to the wine: instead, they allow the wine to mature and develop without outside help. The result is a wine showing true characters developed from the wine itself, as intended by the winemaker.
- Because there will be no leakage of gases through the screwcap wine seal, your wines will cellar equally well in either upright or horizontal positions.
- We are committed to bringing our wines to you in the best possible condition. And we know that the only way to do this confidently is to seal every bottle with a screwcap wine seal.

Strong stuff – but they mean it! If you have shares in the natural cork industry, now is the time to pull the plug.

The Mont Tauch co-operative in France's Languedoc make some of the region's top bargains
– stockists include Majestic and Tesco

The pick of the year

No doubt whatsoever about my Retailer of the Year – Marks & Spencer. And there is an encouraging number of high-scoring wines this year. Listed here are the highest scorers under the £5 mark.

Red wines

11

Miranda Rovalley Ridge Petit Verdot 2000	£4.49	*Tesco*

10/11

Sainsbury's Vin de Pays d'Oc Rouge	£2.99	*Sainsbury's*
Grenache Noir Old Vines Vin de Pays Catalan 2000	£4.99	*Marks & Spencer*

10

Safeway Rhône Valley Red 2001	£2.99	*Safeway*
Co-op Vin de Pays Merlot	£3.49	*Co-op*
Cabernet Sauvignon, Limouxins, 2001	£3.49	*Majestic*
Coldridge Estate Shiraz Cabernet, 2001	£3.79	*Majestic*
L'Enclos Domeque Syrah Malbec 2000	£3.99	*Safeway*
Mosaique Merlot 2000	£3.99	*Oddbins*
Quiltro Cabernet Sauvignon 1999	£3.99	*Oddbins*
Tesco Finest Corbières Reserve La Sansoure 2000	£3.99	*Tesco*
Gold Label Cabernet Sauvignon 2001	£4.49	*Marks & Spencer*
Somerfield Argentine Sangiovese 2001	£4.49	*Somerfield*
Albera Barbera d'Asti 2000	£4.99	*Safeway*
Domaine du Colombier Chinon 2001	£4.99	*Sainsbury's*
Goats do Roam 2001	£4.99	*Co-op, Majestic, Oddbins, Somerfield, Waitrose*

Inycon Merlot 2000	£4.99	*Safeway, Somerfield, Tesco*
Inycon Syrah 2000	£4.99	*Sainsbury's, Tesco*
Valréas Domaine de la Grande Bellane 1999	£4.99	*Co-op*

White wines

10

Oakley Adams Verdelho 2000	£2.99	*Aldi*
Asda Manzanilla Sherry	£3.87	*Asda*
Moscato Piemonte, Cantine Gemma, 2001	£3.89	*Oddbins*
Château de Valombré 2001	£3.99	*Aldi*
Bodega Lurton Pinot Gris 2001	£4.49	*Waitrose*
La Mouline Viognier 2000	£4.99	*Safeway*
Piesporter Goldtröpfchen Kabinett, Weller-Lehnert, 1996	£4.99	*Majestic*

One of several very successful Co-op own brands, this sunny ripe red bursting with hedgerow fruit costs just £3.49

The retailers

In this edition, I have focused attention on the largest national retailers. The Big Five of Asda, Safeway, Sainsbury's, Somerfield and Tesco are here in depth. So is Waitrose which, in spite of confining its shops so strictly on a geographical basis (namely England's high-earning southern regions), has easily the widest and most exciting range of any of the supermarkets – and offers the entire list to mail-order customers nationwide.

Also here for the first time ever is Aldi, the German-owned 'no-frills' chain of small-scale, bargain supermarkets. Aldi kindly sent me samples of its small range of wines, and I have been very impressed with some of them – for quality as well as price.

I have not included regional supermarkets (Waitrose aside), nor any high-street merchant besides Oddbins, because none has offered me the chance to taste from a really broad range of their wines and, frankly, none in my opinion has a really broad range of wine anyway.

This is also why the huge First Quench chain is absent from this edition. I know its shops (Thresher, Wine Rack, Victoria Wine and Bottoms Up) are everywhere, but my visits to local branches have not inspired my recommendation.

But to conclude on a high note, Marks & Spencer is back in. The M&S tasting in 2002 was the revelation of the year, and the stores are without doubt one of the best sources of bargain wines – at all price levels – to be found anywhere.

ALDI

I first discovered Aldi supermarkets in France, where their products include amazingly cheap olive oil that is nevertheless of genuinely good quality, and assorted canned foods of a similar price–quality ratio. So it has come as a pleasant surprise to me to discover in the past year that Aldi has 262 stores in the UK – and what's more that they have their own range of wines.

Unlike the other well-known European 'no-frills' chain, Lidl, Aldi's products are all its own, and, says Aldi, these own-brands are of a quality that 'matches that of leading brands'.

Aldi has more than 5,000 stores across the world, so it must have monster buying power. The stores are relatively small, with about 800 distinct own-label products including the small wine range of 30 or so different regular lines.

I have tasted just about all the wines, and can say that among them are several real bargains. The prices are very low, but in many cases this is at no cost to quality. I thoroughly recommend wine enthusiasts to seek out the nearest branch and try some of these. If you don't know where your nearest Aldi is, ring the Store Location Line on 08705 134262 or look on the web at **www.aldi-stores.co.uk**.

Smoothness and spice are among the markers of this bargain Costières de Nîmes from Aldi, well priced at £3.99

RED WINES

AUSTRALIA

£2.99   8   Badgers Creek Shiraz-Cabernet

Just short of thin, this is OK for the money – Aussie wine at £2.99 is a rare thing indeed

£3.99   8   Oakley Adams Merlot Shiraz 2000

Soft, squishy morello fruit with a trace of sweetness some will like (and some might not) makes for an interesting glassful

£3.99   9/10   Woodbury Cabernet Sauvignon 2001

Solid dark-fruited Cabernet has a likeable liquorice centre and seems very good value for money

CHILE

£2.99   9   Chilean Cabernet Sauvignon

Perfectly good, characteristic blackcurranty light Cabernet at an impressively low price

FRANCE

£3.99   9/10   Château de Valombré 2000

Vanilla is the prominent flavour in this velvety good-value Costières de Nîmes, but the guts and spice for which the AC is rightly known do shine through

SPAIN

£2.99   9   Campo Lindo Crianza 1998

Very light oaky red in the Spanish manner holds together quite well – improved on retaste the day after, interestingly

AUSTRALIA

£2.99 10 Oakley Adams Verdelho 2000

Extraordinary gold-coloured dry white from Riverland district has emphatic vegetal style with a marked petroliness, modest alcohol (12%) and genuine interest – as well as a remarkably low price

£3.99 9 Woodbury Verdelho Chardonnay 2000

Nice tropical note in this interesting blend – seems cheap at the price

BULGARIA

£2.49 9 Budavar Chardonnay 2000

Mild-mannered clean screwcap chardy without fault and very cheap

CHILE

£2.99 9/10 Chilean Sauvignon Blanc

Fresh and lively typical Sauvignon of real quality – terrific value

FRANCE

£3.99 10 Château de Valombré 2001

Marvellous balance of clean green fruit and creamy-oaky richness in this lush dry white from the esteemed appellation of Costières de Nîmes – a great bargain

£3.99 9 Hooting Owl Sauvignon Blanc 2001

Vin de Pays d'Oc has the melon-fruit more associated with, say, South African Sauvignon, but a refreshing glassful just the same

SOUTH AFRICA

£2.49 9/10 Cape Spring Chenin Blanc 2001

A real surprise wine – the nose and first taste are distinctly Sauvignon in character, giving way to a pleasant light dry refresher that belies this very low price

PERSONAL NOTES:

....
....
....
....
....
....
....
....
....
....
....
....

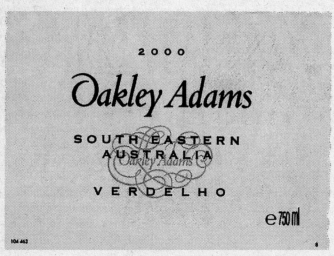

A truly remarkable wine at £2.99 from Aldi, this Australian curio has gold colour and delicious 'petrolly' flavour

ASDA

The former Associated Dairies supermarket chain, now part of the world's biggest retailer, US giant Wal-Mart, is said to be the fastest-growing of all retailers in Britain. It has 254 outlets throughout the UK – fewer than half the number of branches of Sainsbury's or Tesco – but is expected to overtake Sainsbury's before long in terms of sales.

I find the wine range at Asda impressive, but bewildering. There are hordes of the usual ubiquitous brands from Australia and America at the same price (give or take a penny or two) as everywhere else. But there is also an ill-defined range of exclusive own-label wines, many of which are of inspired quality and much cheaper than their approximate counterparts in the other four of the Big Five supermarkets.

As part of a company with huge buying power – Wal-Mart's annual sales are £150 billion – Asda no doubt has considerable negotiating strength when it comes to dealing with suppliers worldwide. The chain reckons that its merchandise, based on a sample of 1,600 products, is on average 12 per cent cheaper than among its major rivals.

So, if you're a particularly price-sensitive shopper for wine, Asda merits a look. In common with other supermarkets, it offers a discount of 5 per cent on 'bulk' buys – which in its case means five or more bottles of wine (including vermouth and fortified wine) priced at £2.50 or above. And, again in common with the competition, Asda does regular promotions on both branded and own-label wines. These are often advertised in the press – and the discounts are sometimes dramatic.

I have tasted a much smaller selection from this chain than from the others, because Asda doesn't offer organised tastings to wine writers (well, to this wine writer anyway) so the wines mentioned here are either from among the 20-odd bottles sent to me when I requested samples or are wines I've bought from the stores in the last year or so.

RED WINES

ARGENTINA

£2.97	9	Asda Argentinian Red	*Perennial lightweight red is consistently good value at this low price*
£3.79	9/10	Asda Argentinian Bonarda 2001	*Delicious bramble-nosed soft but trim Italian-style spaghetti wine at a very good price*
£3.99	7	Asda Argentine Sangiovese 2000	*Has a certain nutty bite, but rather dilute*
£4.49	8	Far Flung Cabernet Merlot 2000	*Plenty of blackcurranty concentration and grip*
£4.99	9	Argento Malbec 2000	*Dark, dense and liquorous wine by excellent Nicolas Catena – to drink with food*

AUSTRALIA

£3.49	9	Asda Karalta Shiraz Cabernet 2000	*Not as vividly fruity as the 1999 vintage but still a good, round glassful at this price*
£3.99	9	Mighty Murray Red 2000	*Dubious name but a very decent jam-scented middleweight (though 14% alcohol) food wine at a keen price*
£6.93	9	Peter Lehmann Clancy's 2000	*A mix of four different grape varieties makes for a poised, Bordeaux-like (and distinctly un-Aussie) mature-tasting balanced wine*

CHILE

£3.29	9	Asda Chilean Red	*Lightweight but fully formed non-vintage soft red is a bargain*
£4.97	9	Asda Cabernet Sauvignon Reserva 2000	*Robust and rounded oaked wine has good blackcurrant character*
£4.98	9/10	Cono Sur Pinot Noir 2001	*Great raspberry whiff off this sunny, earthy and concentrated typical Pinot with lots of grunt (14% alcohol)*

| £4.99 | 8 | Terramater Zinfandel Shiraz 2000 | *Soft-fruit style delivers beguiling mix of spice and strawberry* |

FRANCE

| £2.99 | 9 | Asda Merlot Vin de Pays d'Oc | *Brambly, slightly lean but ripe cheapie of creditable quality* |
| £4.99 | 9 | Buzet Cuvée 44 1998 | *I keep coming across this brand, and keep liking it – warm and ripe with peppery hint* |

ITALY

£2.77	9	Asda Sicilian Red 2000	*Tastes just the same as all other supermarket own-label red Sicilians and, as such, good – and even cheaper than most*
£2.99	8	La Vis Merlot 2000	*Simple brambly lightweight to throw down with the spaghetti*
£3.47	8	Trulli Primitivo del Salento 2000	*Light in colour but dark in intense fruit – a food wine*
£3.99	9/10	Asda Chianti Colli Senesi 2000	*Very successful indeed – concentrated mocha-and-cherry style with lively fruit, grippy finish*
£4.99	8	Pendulum Zinfandel 1999	*Gilt-bottled Puglian plummy-raisiny winter wine*

PORTUGAL

| £4.79 | 8 | Cataplana 1999 | *A light (but 13.5% alcohol) and squishy-minty red-fruit glugger from the Algarve* |
| £6.98 | 9/10 | Late Bottled Vintage Port, Smith Woodhouse, 1995 | *Properly rounded and relishable well-knit port with silky appeal – this is much cheaper than equivalent supermarket LBVs and a true bargain* |

SPAIN

| £2.99 | 9/10 | Asda Tempranillo 2001 | *Bouncy strawberry-fruit refresher is vigorously delicious* |

WHITE WINES

ARGENTINA

£2.99	9	Asda Argentinian White	*Very cheap soft 'tropical-fruit' dry white is a respectable party wine*
£3.49	9/10	Asda Argentinian Torrontes 2000	*Whiff of spicy-grapey Muscat about this fruit-salad of a wine*
£4.97	9	Far Flung Viognier 2001	*Nice weight to this peachy soft but refreshing dry white with 13.5% alcohol*

AUSTRALIA

£3.48	9	Asda Karalta Chardonnay	*Assertively oaked SE Australian wine has impactful, almost petrolly fruit – a lot of flavour for the price*
£3.62	9	Asda Karalta Semillon 2000	*Cheaper than last year's vintage and about as good – distinct peachy-honey nose on a dry fresh fruit*
£4.49	9	Lindemans Cawarra Unoaked Chardonnay 2001	*Cleverly contrived big brand has purity and creaminess and impressive citrus finish*
£4.99	9/10	Cranswick Estate Marsanne 2000	*Exotic aroma to this gold-coloured pineapple-and-vanilla confection*
£4.99	9	Pendulum Chardonnay 2000	*'Concept' wine in a weird silvered bottle looks a lot better in the glass – generous gold colour and rich vanilla-coconutty style*
£5.94	8	Brown Bros Late Harvested Orange Muscat & Flora 2001	*Pricey but pretty good blossom-perfumed sticky*

CHILE

£2.99	8	Asda Chilean White	*Soft simple dry white has price as its principal merit*
£4.79	9	35 South Sauvignon Blanc 2001	*Fresh and crisp, perhaps lacking the focus I remember from the previous vintage*

FRANCE

£3.23 7 Chardonnay Vin de Pays du
Jardin de la France 2000

Slim-flavoured Loire white

£4.99 9 Denis Marchais Hand-Picked
Vouvray 1999

Blossomy nose on this lush but zesty Loire dry white

£6.98 9 Asda Chablis 2001

Decent stony wine in recognisable Chablis style

GERMANY

£3.92 8 Kendermann Riesling
Kabinett 1999

Rightly popular brand is crisp and, I suppose, appealingly un-German

£3.99 9 Devil's Rock Riesling 2000

Looks Australian but this racy Rhine wine is crisp, dry and definitely German

ITALY

£3.99 9 Asda La Vis Pinot Grigio 2001

Another good vintage in the aromatic, smoky style with easy fresh softness

£4.29 9 Marc Xero Chardonnay

Creamy-fruit dry style comes in a frosted bottle

SOUTH AFRICA

£3.47 9/10 African Cape Chardonnay 2001

Pretty good – a well-put-together tropical fruit style with ripeness (13% alcohol) and sunny fruit

SPAIN

£3.87 10 Asda Manzanilla Sherry

Absolutely cracking value – a tangy ultra-dry sherry to compare with brands at twice the price

PERSONAL NOTES:

....
....
....
....
....
....
....
....
....
....
....
....

Spicy-grapey Muscat-perfumed dry white is one of Asda's real own-label bargains at £3.49

CO-OP

As wine merchants go, the Co-op can hardly lay claim to the smartest image. But as wine ranges go, I can assure you that its 1,841 licensed stores have one of the most interesting to be found anywhere.

The organisation has taken its wines seriously ever since hiring Dr Arabella Woodrow, formerly of Harveys of Bristol, in the 1980s to put together a completely new list including exclusive new 'own-label' brands. Dr Woodrow succeeded in this task brilliantly, and her successor Paul Bastard – who has heard all the jokes – now maintains the same high standards.

The upshot is that even in small Co-op branches you will find a decent choice of real quality wines, and in the 'superstores' the selection will match the likes of Sainsbury's and Tesco, if not for sheer numbers of wines, certainly for genuine variety.

A feature of all the own-brand wines is their back labels. It is the Co-op's policy to state all the ingredients in their own wines, and the back labels look very busy on account of it. Co-op Malbec-Bonarda, for example, boasts this ingredient list: 'Grapes. Tartaric acid, Preservative (Sulphur Dioxide), Antioxidant (Ascorbic acid). Made using: Yeast, Potassium bitartrate, Yeast Nutrient (Diammonium phosphate). Cleared using: Bentonite, Gelatine.'

Nothing sinister among this lot, I promise, but in an ingredient-conscious world, the Co-op should be congratulated on this kind of openness. No other supermarket – and certainly no other wine retailer, including organic wine specialists – is similarly upfront, and I hope the Co-op is winning lots of new customers on account of it.

The company has its own dedicated website for wine shoppers who prefer home-delivery. It gives details of current special offers as well as 'a selection' from the full list of 500 or so different wines and spirits. Visit it at: **www.co-opdrinks2u.com.**

RED WINES

ARGENTINA

£3.69	9	Co-op Argentine Malbec-Bonarda 1999	*Good value Italian-style own-brand has bright flavours and neat finish – good for drinking with pasta*
£3.99	9	Adiseño Tempranillo 2001	*Mild-mannered soft red has a whiff of raspberry*
£3.99	8	Graffigna Shiraz-Cabernet Sauvignon 1999	*Slightly tough blend, just as apparently overripe as the previous vintage, so the style is presumably intended*
£3.99	9	Lost Pampas 2000	*Co-op own brand has edgy-young, glyceriney style from Cabernet and Malbec grapes*
£4.99	9	Argento Malbec 2000	*Dark, dense and liquorous wine by excellent Nicolas Catena – to drink with food*

AUSTRALIA

£4.29	9/10	Co-op Grenache 2001	*Jammy monster (14% alcohol) from SE Australia has dark charm, delivering a lot of flavour for the money – unusually good value for an Aussie red*
£4.29	8	Co-op Merlot 2001	*Solid one-dimensional wine with no particular faults and 13.5% alcohol*
£4.99	9	Lindemans Cawarra Shiraz Cabernet 2000	*Decent spicy wine is light by Aussie standards but satisfying*
£6.99	9	Rosemount Shiraz Cabernet 2000	*Juicy and spicy berry-fruit dark style is relishably brambly*

CHILE

£3.79	5	Long Slim Red Cabernet-Merlot	*Thin and stringy wine camouflaged under an eyecatching label*
£3.99	8	Four Rivers Cabernet Sauvignon 1999	*Strong, distinctly blackcurranty and slightly tough*
£4.99	8	Co-op Fair Trade Chilean Carmenère 2000	*Decent middleweight blackcurranty wine is made by fair-trading Los Robles co-operative*
£4.99	9	Santa Carolina Merlot 2000	*Dense black-cherry smoothie from a dependable producer*
£4.99	8	Terramater Malbec 1999	*Direct punchy dark fruit is uncomplicatedly pleasing*
£4.99	8	Terramater Zinfandel-Syrah 2000	*Soft, sweetish style evokes strawberries – and white pepper*

FRANCE

£2.99	9/10	Rhône Valley Red Wine	*Great value, this Côtes du Luberon has the warm and faintly peppery ripeness of pricier Rhône wines – satisfying stuff*
£3.49	10	Co-op Vin de Pays Merlot	*Amazing quality at this price – a sunny ripe red bursting with hedgerow fruit and with a perfectly balanced finish*
£3.99	9/10	Co-op Vin de Pays d'Oc Cabernet Sauvignon	*One of an impressively consistent new range of vin de pays introduced in 2001, this is well balanced between sturdiness and juiciness with lush cassis fruit*
£4.99	9	Co-op French Organic Merlot Syrah	*Neat marriage of silk and spice in this ripe vin de pays from the new organic range*

£4.99	9	Château Pierrousselle 2000	*A really decent fully formed claret with middle weight but rounded style – unusual quality and character for Bordeaux at this price*
£4.99	10	Valréas Domaine de la Grande Bellane 1999	*Intensely ripe and spicy top-of-the-range organic Côtes du Rhône Villages at a great price*

ITALY

£2.99	9/10	Co-op Sicilian Red Wine	*I can't recommend this too highly – maybe it comes from the same mysterious source as all other supermarket Sicilian reds, but in its softly fruity, warm, cherry-topped style it's an outstanding buy at this price*
£3.79	9/10	Co-op Chianti 2000	*A very pleasant surprise – cheap Chianti that actually evokes the true character of this inimitable style, complete with almondy scent, juicy fruit and label by Botticelli*
£4.99	9/10	Inycon Merlot 1999	*Nice spearmint waft off this handsomely coloured Sicilian wine with dark, peppery fruit – gripping stuff with 14.5% alcohol*
£4.99	9	Melini Chianti 1999	*Lightish but firm fruit with the proper nutskin-dry finish and an evocative cherry whiff in a big-brand Chianti that's unusually good value for money*
£5.49	9	Otto Santi Chianti Classico 1998	*Reasonable price for this cherry-fruit and grippy Chianti with plenty of concentration*

PORTUGAL

£3.29   9   Ramada 2000

Whiff of clove oil and honey-minty centre to the lightweight fruit – an intriguing cheapie from Estremadura region

£3.99   9   Terra Boa 1999

Sweet nose but keenly edged dark fruit to this workmanlike red from Tras-Os-Montes region

£4.49   8   Big Baga

Gimmicky packaging of an ordinary wine from Portugal's indigenous Baga grape

SOUTH AFRICA

£4.99   10   Goats do Roam 2001

Silly name-take on Côtes du Rhône but this rightly popular brand just seems to get better and better with each vintage – lush, strawberry-scented, ripe and sunny red with guts (13.5% alcohol)

SPAIN

£3.99   9   Berberana Dragon Tempranillo

Rather a good, cheap oaky middleweight from a famed Rioja producer

£4.49   8   Viña Albali Tinto Reserva 1997

Emphatically vanilla-oaked mature Valdepeñas is lightish but satisfying

USA

£3.99   6   Laid Back Ruby 2000

Lured by the gaudy packaging into this gaudy Californian 'Ruby Cabernet' only to find it a rather dilute confection

WHITE WINES

ARGENTINA

£3.99 9 Rio de Plata Torrontes 2000

Grapey-soft but breezily crisp aperitif wine or Asian food matcher

AUSTRALIA

£3.99 7 Butterfly Ridge Sauvignon-Chenin Blanc 2000

Cheap fresh lightweight for parties

£4.49 9 Hardy's Stamp Series Chardonnay-Semillon 2000

Catch-all big-brand blend delivers clean Chardonnay with a mild caramel twist – really rather likeable

CHILE

£4.99 9 Santa Carolina Sauvignon Blanc 2001

Successfully crisp and aromatic Sauvignon has unchallenging acidity but genuine interest – and 13.5% alcohol

FRANCE

£3.99 8 Co-op Vin de Pays

Safe, soft dry white – and 'vegetarian'

GERMANY

£3.69 8 Co-op Four Rs 1999

New wave (i.e. un-Liebfraumilch-like) grapey-fresh dryish white

£3.99 9 Devil's Rock Riesling 2000

Looks Australian but this racy Rhine wine is crisp, dry and definitely German

ITALY

£3.99 9 Orvieto Classico 2000

Pleasing herbaceous style to a softly refreshing dry white

£4.49 9/10 Trulli Chardonnay 2000

Good extra-ripe appley-oily Salento (heel of Italy) varietal

£4.99 9/10 Inycon Chardonnay 2001

Good new vintage of this super Sicilian has plenty of colour and appley Chardonnay character – and 13.5% alcohol

PORTUGAL

£4.99   **8**   **Fiuza Chardonnay 2000**   *Dried-fruit note in this unusual rich but dry Chardonnay*

PERSONAL NOTES:

....

....

....

....

....

....

....

....

....

....

The herbaceous dry whites of Orvieto in Italy's Umbria region can be bland, but this Co-op bargain (£3.99) stands out

MAJESTIC

 I had the honour of attending the opening of Majestic's hundredth branch in the summer of 2002, in Dorchester, Dorset. All the company's management turned out for the occasion, and I must say they looked pretty pleased with themselves.

It's taken the chain 21 years from the day the initial two branches, in Battersea and Wood Green in London, were bought by a couple of shrewd investment bankers to evolve into what is now a major national merchant.

The only member of the original crew at Majestic still with the company, buying director Tony Mason, is happy to admit that an expansion from two to a hundred branches is a modest-enough achievement over a period when some retailers have grown out of all recognition – or gone spectacularly bust. But he points out that the business is very picky indeed about choosing sites – which have to conform to several crucial criteria as well as be affordable.

The new Majestic at Dorchester sums up these qualifications neatly. It's close to the town centre, it has customer parking, and its oceans of space (it's a former car showroom) include a well-equipped 'tasting counter' for trying out a generous number of wines on sample. There's a lot of wine, stacked in canyons six cases high, but adequate manoeuvring space in which to steer round the supermarket trolleys that feature in every branch.

Majestic, as presumably everyone knows by now, sells on a wholesale basis only. This is what gave it its original edge. As Tony Mason points out: 'It was simply a quirk of the law back in 1981 that one of the few kinds of business allowed to stay open all day on Sundays was a wholesale wine merchant.' And for the first few years, before supermarkets lobbied successfully for changes in trading laws, Majestic prospered mightily on Sundays – its second best trading day of the week – and in effect established it as a unique player in a very competitive game.

It does seem that Majestic's 'disadvantage' of being limited only to wholesaling has been turned round completely. The typical customer spends more than £100 per visit, which must make the administration-to-sales ratio very satisfactory indeed. And, because people who buy wine in quantity tend to be the more-adventurous type, they go for quality, too.

And there's quality here in depth. My first stop is always at the German section, where this year there is another inspiring collection of mature Moselles at ridiculously low prices. There's a lot of Bordeaux wine from recent rather mixed vintages, but I find the Burgundy and Rhône ranges much more interesting. Again loads of Loire whites – I've never seen so many Sancerres in one place – and even a large choice from that most neglected French region, Alsace.

Vin de Pays and Italian IGT wines account for most of the £2.99-type bargains but always look out for Majestic's offers on New World wines, which are regularly reduced in 'buy 2 save £1' deals. And if you're a sherry fan, don't miss out on the impressive (and frequently discounted) Hidalgo range.

One area of Britain in which Majestic is not continuing to expand its network is south-east England – within easiest reach of the Channel ports. Wholesaling wine in competition with the *hypermarchés* and booze warehouses across the water is a lost cause. So instead of investing in hugely expensive sites in Kent or East Sussex, Majestic in 2002 spent £4 million on the four-branch Calais business prosaically known as the Wine and Beer Company.

Over time, the shops – two in Calais and one each in Cherbourg and Le Havre – will take on more and more of Majestic's own range, but will retain many of the bog-standard booze-cruise Liebfraumilch and branded wines that have been their mainstay to date. If you're planning a trip you can preview the list and its mass of special offers online either on www.wineandbeer.co.uk or, if French bureaucracy has permitted, on Majestic's own brilliantly ordered site at www.majestic.co.uk. You can even pre-order all the wines you want online, and simply turn up to collect the goods when the time comes.

ARGENTINA

£4.99 9 Argento Malbec 2001

Dark, dense and liquorous wine by excellent Nicolas Catena – to drink with food

£6.99 9/10 Carrascal Cavas de Weinert 1997

Still a youthful purple colour in spite of its age, this dark-hearted red from Malbec, Cabernet and Merlot grapes is startling similar to a claret – and a good claret at that

£8.99 9/10 Catena Cabernet Sauvignon 1997

If you're going to push the boat out on an Argentinian wine, go for this one – sublime, silky-minty Cabernet of unforgettable style

AUSTRALIA

£3.79 10 Coldridge Estate Shiraz Cabernet 2001

True Cabernet character with cassis-essence fruit – real wine that's really fun and amazingly cheap

£3.79 9/10 Coldridge Estate Merlot 2001

Simple sweetly ripe black-cherry style to this chunky (13.5% alcohol) slurper

£6.99 9 Oxford Landing Limited Release Shiraz 1999

Powerful peppery nose and warm spicy upfront fruit to suit robust thirsts

£6.99 9/10 Tyrell's Old Winery Pinot Noir

Pale but proper Pinot colour (hint of orange-brown) and a lush strawberry nose ahead of heaps of fruit (and alcohol at 14%) – this is an exciting wine

£7.49 9 Rosemount Estate Shiraz 2000

Jolly red giant has stacks of roasty fruit

£7.49 10 Tatachilla McLaren Vale Grenache-Shiraz 2001

Gorgeous squashed-fruit nose on this crushed-bramble, lavishly ripe (14.5% alcohol) smoothie

CHILE

£3.79	9	La Mira Cabernet Sauvignon 2000	*Nice cool minty nose on a friendly ripe wine at a good price*
£3.79	8	La Mira Merlot 2000	*Brambly-woody simple cheapie*
£4.99	9/10	Vistasur Cabernet 2000	*Plush cassis-centred Cabernet has silky fruit*
£4.99	9	Vistasur Merlot 2000	*Dark colour is already browning – nice soft ripe style*
£5.99	9	Valdivieso Barrel Selection Merlot 1999	*Keen cutting edge to this vividly fruity red – will go very well with starchy dishes*
£6.49	8	Casa Lapostolle Cabernet Sauvignon 1999	*Dense purple colour, wet nose and mouth-drying tannin but a likeable enough wine that might improve with time*
£6.99	9	Santa Rita Reserva Cabernet Sauvignon 2000	*Pure-fruit blackcurranty wine that's a big improvement on the 1999 vintage*
£7.49	9	Montes Limited Selection Pinot Noir 2000	*Fine earthy Pinot has sleekness and dimension – stands out from the crowd*
£8.99	9	Valdivieso Single Vineyard Reserve Cabernet Franc 1999	*Subtle purply mouth-gripping wine has good balance of ripe fruit and dry edge – should have come on nicely since tasting a year ago*

FRANCE

£2.99	9/10	Domaine de Richard 2001	*Jolly dark purple inky sort of wine has none of the faults of dilution or ersatz sweetness common in wines under £3 – definitely recommended*
£2.99	9/10	Cuvée des Amandiers 2001	*Nice dense Vin de Pays d'Oc with typical leafy Grenache nose (there's 30% per cent in the mix too) and blackberry-jam fruit – another real bargain*

£3.49	10	Cabernet Sauvignon, Limouxins, 2001	*Brilliant value – a home-made-jam-labelled Vin de Pays d'Oc that hits the flavour-balance target bang in the middle for joyful fruitiness and crisp completeness*
£3.99	7	Bourgogne Passetoutgrains 2000	*Bracing earthy-woody cheap burgundy from famed (but not faultless) co-op at Buxy*
£3.99	5	Le Fauve Merlot 2000	*Vin de Pays d'Oc with wild boar motif (a fauve is a wild beast) has disappointingly little flesh on it*
£4.49	9	Corbières Domaine Madelon 2001	*Was £3.99 last year but priced up since, so reduced in score, but a ripe and juicy red with a dark, tarry heart*
£4.49	9	Domaine Plantade Syrah Merlot 2001	*Dense blackberry style and good grip to this decent sunny Vin de Pays d'Oc*
£4.99	9	Costières de Nîmes, Château Guiot, 2001	*Truffley smell on this rustic-tasting but very likeable mildly spicy and tannic middleweight*
£4.99	9/10	Côtes du Rhône Villages Cairanne 2000	*Robust ripe spicy assertive characterful red from a highly rated individual village*
£4.99	7	La Vieille Ferme Côtes du Ventoux 2000	*Raisiny hot nose, a strong but hard wine*
£4.99	8	Mâcon Rouge St Gengoux 2000	*Sunny southern Burgundy red is rather austere*
£4.99	9	Terra Vitis Corbières 2001	*Purple-black with honey-centred nose and corresponding fruit masked by a lot of tannin – will keep well*
£5.49	9/10	Beaumes de Venise La Chapelle Nôtre Dame d'Aubune 2000	*Spicy fruit, dark-hearted, mouth-gripping super-ripe Rhône-village red with 14% alcohol*
£5.49	9	Chinon Les Garous, Couly-Dutheil, 2001	*Characterful leafy densely fruity vigorous Loire red*

£5.49	9	Corbières, Château de Luc, 2000	*Another robust and smooth, white-pepper-tinged wine from this Majestic perennial*
£5.49	10	Mont Tauch Fitou 1999	*Mature, oak-aged Languedoc classic of surpassing quality, midweight, perfumed and poised – and in a frightfully smart bottle*
£6.49	8	Faugères Abbaye Sylva Plana La Closerie 2000	*Dense and deep but still a bit hard, this needs time*
£6.99	8	Château du Trignon Côtes du Rhône Villages Sablet 1999	*Pale slightly woody but well-focused upmarket CDR with 13.5% alcohol*
£7.99	9/10	Château de Gaudou Cuvée Renaissance 1999	*Top Cahors estate's 'revival' oaked red is dense and balanced between smooth vanilla oak and tongue-tingling spice – lovely stuff from the Lot Valley*
£9.49	8	Gigondas, Château du Trignon, 1999	*Pale-coloured but strong (14% alcohol) spicy and concentrated Rhône village red – not cheap, though*

ITALY

£3.49	5	Sangiovese Marche, Marchesini, 2000	*Looks good in its long slim bottle and postage-stamp label but tastes poor with its short thin fruit*
£3.99	9	Valpolicella Terre del Sole, Pasqua, 2000	*Cherry-fruit goes right through this bright young wine with a nutty finish*
£4.49	8	Chianti Casellino, Fratelli Grati, 1999	*Well-coloured light-middleweight with detectable Chianti character*
£4.99	8	Bardolino Cavalchina 2001	*Typical vivid cherry-style light red*
£4.99	8	Valpolicella Classico Santepierre 2000	*Nutty firm cherry-fruit red*
£4.99	9	Copertino Masseria Monaci 1998	*Good solid wine with an earthy – even volcanic – element and proper Italian dry finish*

£4.99 9/10 Sangiovese Syrah, Accademia del Sole Calatrasi, 1999

Velvety colour, spirity-raisiny nose, generous earthy fruit and nutskin finish on this delightful Sicilian, made by an Australian

£5.49 9/10 Rosso Conero Conti Cortesi 1999

Earthy, gripping southern red is a worthy successor to the excellent 1998 vintage

£6.99 9 Selian Carignan Tunisia Calatrasi 1999

Made in Sicily with grapes shipped from Muslim Tunisia by its Australian maker, a dark, minty, softly tannic red of real charm

£7.49 9 Valpolicella Classico Superiore Ripasso La Casetta de Ettore Rignetti 1999

A big, sunny extension of the cherry-fruit Valpolicella theme has lushness and good almondy character

£7.99 8 Chianti Classico Banfi 2000

Cherry-scented pleasantly abrasive Chianti is good, but seems rather expensive

£9.99 9 Rosso di Montalcino Banfi 1999

Pricey but densely delicious rich wine that really needs a couple more years in bottle to show at its best

NEW ZEALAND

£8.99 9 Delegats Reserve Cabernet Sauvignon 1999

Typical minty Kiwi nose and sleek, silky cool-climate character – this classic New Zealand is distinctive and delicious

PORTUGAL

£4.99 9/10 Duque de Viseu Dão 1999

Mature red already going orange at the edge has lush, sweet eucalyptus nose and ripe fruit – wonderful, distinctive wine

£4.99 8 Monte Velho Tinto 2000

Soft minty middleweight

£6.99 5 Duas Quintas Tinto Douro 1999

Disappointingly light and dilute wine from a region that usually does much better

SOUTH AFRICA

£4.99   10   Goats do Roam 2001

Silly name-take on Côtes du Rhône but this rightly popular brand just seems to get better and better with each vintage – lush, strawberry-scented, ripe and sunny red with guts (13.5% alcohol)

SPAIN

£3.99   9   Dragon Tempranillo 2000

Light but focused soft-fruit red from Rioja giant Berberana

£3.99   9   Protocolo Tinto Dominio de Eguren

Artful, tannic Tempranillo with robust fruit

Cahors wines tend to be little more than imitation claret, but Gaudou makes special stuff, like this one at £7.99 from Majestic

FRANCE

£3.49 9/10 Rosé d'Anjou La Jaglerie 2001   *Very pale onion-skin colour but a delightful soft-fruit, strawberry style that makes for an unusually convincing wine (something rosé rarely is)*

£3.99 8 Côtes du Ventoux Rosé Le Passe Colline 2001   *Rhône rosé has sweet fruit and a curiously harsh acidity – drink very cool*

£4.99 7 Abbaye de Sylva Plana 2001   *A pink Faugères from the Languedoc, of ordinary quality*

£4.99 9 Château Guiot Rosé 2001   *From admirable Costières de Nîmes appellation, a livid magenta colour and taste-bud-gripping lively fruit – good stuff*

ITALY

£4.99 8 Chiaretto Cavalchina Estate 2001   *Very pale pink from Bardolino has pleasing floral nose and refreshing tang*

SPAIN

£5.99 9 Rioja Rosado Muga 2001   *The best of this fairly priced collection of pinks from Majestic, but the most expensive (could be a moral here) – a pink rarity from Rioja with very pale colour but a distinct flavour that can be described only as, well, pink Rioja*

WHITE WINES

ARGENTINA

£5.99	9	Alamos Ridge Chardonnay 1999	*Lush nutty-tangy and inspiringly interesting wine from top Argentine producer Nicolas Catena*

AUSTRALIA

£3.79	9	Coldridge Estate Chardonnay 2001	*Lot of bright fruit for the money*
£4.99	9	Oxford Landing Chardonnay 2001	*Big tropical style to an archetypal Aussie upfront Chardonnay*
£4.99	9/10	Oxford Landing Sauvignon Blanc 2001	*A bit of an Alka Seltzer start to the flavour of this classic Sauvignon – just 11% alcohol, and it works very well*
£4.99	9	Tatachilla Breakneck Creek Chardonnay 2000	*Loads of colour, intriguing green-wood nose, eager flavour*
£5.49	9/10	Barossa Valley Riesling, Bethany, 2001	*Apples and lime nose and fresh fruit follow-up – good value*
£5.99	9	Tatachilla McLaren Vale Sauvignon Semillon 2001	*Lively floral nose and zippy fruit from the grape varieties with which dry white Bordeaux is made – rarely with this sort of panache*
£6.99	9	Rosemount Estate Sauvignon Blanc 2001	*Forceful gripping zesty full-flavoured Sauvignon worth the higher price*

CHILE

£3.99	8	La Mira Chardonnay 2001	*All-purpose budget Chardonnay is clean and rather alcoholic at 14%*
£3.99	8	La Mira Sauvignon Blanc	*Decent middle fruit to this gentle dry white*
£4.99	9	Vistasur Chardonnay 2000	*Well-coloured, bright eggy wine with balance*
£4.99	9	Vistasur Sauvignon Blanc 2001	*Zippy aroma, generous fruit, shy on acidity but satisfying*

£5.99	9	Montes Reserve Sauvignon Blanc 2001	*Masses of gooseberry and asparagus on nose, an authentically fresh Sauvignon*
£6.49	6	Santa Rita Reserva Sauvignon 2000	*Famous estate's Sauvignon is not as exciting as before – rather flat*
£6.99	9	Casa Lapostolle Chardonnay 2000	*Splendidly over-the-top golden super-ripe Chardonnay*

FRANCE

£2.99	9	Cuvée de Richard 2001	*Clean refresher from Toulouse is from boring Ugni Blanc grapes but contrives to be a pleasant, low-acidity dry glugger*
£2.99	8	Cuvée Elise Demi Sec 2001	*Soft sweet-smelling Toulouse white is dry, really, in the mouth – quite clean and refreshing*
£3.99	9	Fortant Dry Muscat 2001	*Recognisable Muscat table-grape flavour in a fresh and bright Vin de Pays d'Oc*
£4.49	8	Domaine Plantade Chardonnay-Viognier 2001	*Whiff of 'tropical' fruit on this softie from Languedoc*
£4.49	8	Les Fontanelles Viognier 2001	*Nice gold colour to a Vin de Pays d'Oc with rather slight softness*
£4.99	9/10	Domaine Caillaubert Sauvignon 2001	*Don't worry about the wet nose – this is a cracking, crisp Sauvignon of real character from Gascony*
£5.49	9/10	Les Grands Rochers Chardonnay 2000	*Well-coloured extravagant Vin de Pays d'Oc convincingly imitates buttery burgundy style*
£5.49	8	Reuilly Les Milets Joseph Mellot 2000	*Vegetal nose and prickly fruit to this interesting green-fruit Loire Sauvignon*
£5.99	7	Laroche Grande Cuvée 'L' Chardonnay 2000	*Oaky New World-style Vin de Pays d'Oc*

£5.99	9	Quincy Le Rimonet Joseph Mellot 2001	*Elusive but distinct Sauvignon nose to a tangy wine with vigour and length – good substitute for much pricier neighbour Sancerre*
£5.99	9	Vouvray Demi-Sec, Domaine Bourillon d'Orléans, 2001	*Lush Loire white is softly honeyed and memorable*
£6.49	9	Reuilly, Henri Beurdin, 2000	*Interesting custard whiff off a crisp dry Sauvignon with a lush twang – quality wine*
£6.99	9	Rully Blanc La Bergerie, Dupasquier, 2000	*Sweet-oaky nose and rather luscious Chardonnay fruit – a pretty decent burgundy at this price*
£8.99	9	Alsace Tokay Pinot Gris, Bott-Geyl, 2000	*Gold-coloured, lush, spicy, smoky wine of great character*
£8.99	8	Chablis Vocoret 2001	*Flinty, classic Chablis but a tad pricey*
£8.99	9/10	Alsace Gewürztraminer, Beblenheim 2000	*Exotic gold wine with smoke, lychee and spice*

GERMANY

£3.99	9	Piesporter Michelsberg Riesling 2000	*Basic off-dry Riesling from Zimmermann Graeff has welcome apple freshness and 8.5% alcohol*
£4.49	9/10	Riesling Ruppertsberg Pfalz 2000	*Fresh, lively Moselle has a lush hint of toffee apple in the middle fruit and 11% alcohol*
£4.99	10	Piesporter Goldtröpfchen Kabinett, Weller-Lehnert, 1996	*Lush, complete Riesling has more honey notes and bigger, softer fruit than expected in a Kabinett – fabulous wine with 8.5% alcohol*
£4.99	9/10	Urziger Würzgarten Kabinett, Christoffel Prüm, 1991	*More than a decade old, but a wine full of lively Riesling fruit and a mere 7.5% alcohol*
£5.49	9/10	Trierer Deutschherrenberg Spätlese 1997	*Grand gold colour, generous nectar hints and racy Riesling fruit – sublime wine with just 7.5% alcohol*

£5.99 9/10 Urziger Würzgarten Spätlese,   *Marvellous match of richness with*
             Christoffel Prüm, 1992   *apple freshness in this fine autumnal*
                                               Moselle – at 8% alcohol

ITALY

£4.49 9 Lugana La Carega, Sartori, 2000   *Gooseberry-floral nose, intense*
                                            mineral fruit – characterful wine

£4.49 8 Pinot Grigio del Veneto,   *Light dry wine with hint of brine*
          Pasqua, 2001

£4.99 8 Bianco di Custoza Cavalchina   *Green-fruit nose on a fresh, light dry*
          2001   *white*

£4.99 8 Orvieto Classico Secco   *Clean-tasting light dry white*
          Barberani 2001

£4.99 9 Soave Classico Santepietre 2000   *Lemony note to this fresh dry wine*
                                            gives it an edge over usual Soave

£4.99 9 Verdicchio dei Castelli di Jesi   *Creamy nose on this fresh, flinty – if*
          Coste del Molino 2001   *anonymous – dry wine*

£6.49 9 Soave Classico Ca'Visco   *Lots of interest and dimension in this*
          Superiore, Coffele, 2001   *upmarket Soave – memorable citric*
                                            edge

£8.49 8 Gavi di Gavi Late Picked Villa   *Famed Piedmont off-dry wine has*
          Lanata 2001   *herbaceous, exotic depths – scores for*
                                            interest rather than value

NEW ZEALAND

£6.99 9 Oyster Bay Sauvignon Blanc 2001 *Lively briny superfresh Marlborough*
                                           classic – reasonable price

SOUTH AFRICA

£6.99 9 Zondernaam Sauvignon Blanc   *Nettley nose and crisp focused fruit*
          2001   *in this eager Stellenbosch wine*

SPAIN

£3.99 9 Protocolo Blanco Dominio de   *Faintly woody but nevertheless fresh*
          Eguren 2000   *oxidised-style dry white – somehow*
                                            very Spanish, and none the worse for
                                            that

| £5.99 | 9 | Cosme Palacio Rioja Blanco 1999 | *Big colour and creamy vanillin nose on this extravagant old-fashioned dry-but-rich wine* |
| £7.99 | 8 | Albariño Rias Baixas, Martin Codax, 2001 | *Trendy wine is vivid and zingy with prickly appeal but some might say rather expensive* |

PERSONAL NOTES:

....

....

....

....

....

....

....

....

....

....

....

Sauvignon from this Loire AC is a keenly priced and delicious substitute for expensive Sancerre – this one is £5.49 at Majestic

MARKS & SPENCER

Definitely the wine retailer of the year. The wines (along with the clothes, I gather) have been utterly transformed. Gone is the St Michael brand of old, but M&S still maintains its policy of selling only its own wines – specially made for the company by producers worldwide and bearing the label declaration 'Exclusive and unique to Marks & Spencer'.

At Marks's headquarters in London to taste about 70 wines from a range that has grown to a total of 350, I must admit I had moments of difficulty believing where I was. From nowhere, M&S has moved, as far as I am concerned, to the very front among wine retailers.

The quality of the wines sought out by the young buying team, who spend a third of their time in the vineyards and wineries, is impressive enough, but the fact that so many of these new wines are so reasonably priced is a revelation, too. M&S food products may be the best of their kind but – let's be honest – they are not exactly cheap. But the wines – plenty of them definitely as exceptional as the lavish foods – are genuine bargains by any standard.

It cheered me up immensely to chat to the people at Marks. One of the buyers, a young and faintly Byronic chap whom I took to be an Anglo–Italian until I discovered his name was Gerd Stepp and he came from Germany's Rheinpfalz wine region, impressed me hugely with his enthusiasm for the new range. He's worked at Marks for just two years, and has clearly had a wonderful time sourcing new wines not just from Germany but in Italy (where he was a winemaker in his last job) and elsewhere.

Gerd told me that under the regime of M&S wine suprema Jane Masters MW, he and his colleagues are able to get out and find truly individual winemakers. They don't have to be big producers, and quantities of wine bought can be as low as 300 cases. As he enthused about the growers he had met, it soon becomes clear why this was the wine tasting of the year.

M&S is unique in having only its own wines – not a drop of Jacob's Creek, Blossom Hill or Gallo gargle anywhere in sight. Now that M&S's 'unique and exclusive' wines have reached such new heights, the time has come to beat a path to its door.

AUSTRALIA

£4.49 9/10 The Jackeroo Shiraz Grenache 2001

Quite pale and purply but a deliciously ripe and robust young wine (13.5% alcohol) of unusual interest among Aussie reds in this price range

£4.99 9 Desert Edge Cabernet Merlot 2000

Stalky whiff to an almost austere wine with straight purity and liveliness of fruit

£4.99 9/10 Wattchow's Landing Shiraz Mataro 2000

Big, rich, tarry and delicious lively wine

£5.99 9 Hermits Hill Durif 2000

Simple old-fashioned and very likeable oaked smoothie

£6.99 9/10 Snapper Cove Cabernet Merlot 1999

Extraordinary wine bears close resemblance to a mature and rather grand claret – terrific stuff

£6.99 9/10 The Avenues Merlot 2000

Superb black-cherry and coffee nose on this dark-fruit cracker with a plain-chocolate heart to the flavour and rich, lingering finish – well worth splashing out on

£7.49 9/10 Claremont Shiraz Malbec 1998

Dense velvet colour and packed with gripping fruit, a lavish ripe (14% alcohol) oaked wine in mid-development – serious quality

£7.99 9/10 Dorrien Estate Bin 442 Shiraz 2000

Dark liquorice-hearted monster (14% alcohol) with exciting richness and structure

CHILE

£4.99 8 Casa Leona Syrah 2001

Light in weight but not short of jammy fruit

£6.99 9 Casa Leona Merlot 2001

Chunky chocolatey oaked wine of impressive density and ripeness (14% alcohol) very much needs decanting to show off its best

FRANCE

£2.99 9/10 Domaine St Pierre 2001

Likeable confectionery nose on this cleverly softened Vin de Pays de L'Hérault – much better wine than the price might suggest

£3.99 9/10 Saumur Réserve Jules Peron 2001

Pale Loire red is utterly distinctive with its leafy Cabernet Franc nose and vigorous young soft-tannic fruit

£4.49 10 Gold Label Cabernet Sauvignon 2001

Good dense colour, lovely blueberry and cream whiff and handsome pure-fruit, gripping style in this astounding Vin de Pays d'Oc

£4.49 7 Touraine Gamay, Jacky Marteau, 2001

Basic raspy Loire Gamay – I much prefer the original Beaujolais version

£4.99 9 Château du Parc 2001

Raw colour to this Languedoc red has corresponding burnt-edged, tannic flavour – obviously a quality wine

£4.99 10/11 Grenache Noir Old Vines Vin de Pays Catalan 2000

Rich, sunburnt nose with distinct raspberry note on this concentrated super-ripe massive wine (14.5% alcohol) in a very smart bottle – brilliant

£6.50 9 Château de Surville Costières de Nîmes 2000

Dark-hearted wine with a spicy nose and massively flavoursome fruit

£6.99 9 Château Gallais Bellevue 1999

Sweetly oaked cassis-fruit Médoc (Bordeaux) is very approachable

£6.99 9 Chinon René Couly 1996

Dark, ripe morello nose on a still-grippy mature Loire red – a good example of a distinctive wine style

£7.99	9	Bourgogne Jerôme Sordet 2000	Lightweight but structured young burgundy at a fair price
£7.99	9/10	Rasteau Côtes du Rhône Villages 2000	Gorgeous dark complex wine that seduces from the first spicy whiff – definitely worth the money
£9.99	9/10	Hautes Côtes de Nuits Genevrières 2000	Lush sweet strawberry and white pepper whiff on this superb ready-to-drink wine – probably as good as burgundy gets at under ten quid
£9.99	9	Terre du Lion St Julien 1997	Posh claret is mature and glowing with pure elegant ripeness – good value

ITALY

| £3.99 | 9/10 | Reggiano Rosso 2001 | Sweet 'lambrusco' perfume to this light-hearted crunchily delicious young soft-fruit red to drink cool |
| £8.99 | 8 | Basilica Caffagio Chianti Classico 2000 | Typically expensive Chianti has luxury smoothness as well as characteristic pleasingly abrasive fruit |

PORTUGAL

£3.99	9	Safra Nova Castelao 2000	Straight young lively and distinctive Ribatejo red with juicy fruit
£4.99	9	Solorico Aragones 2000	Very dark, dense Ribatejo red with gripping, plummy fruit
£5.99	9/10	Vinha Padre Pedro 1998	Unusual Ribatejo red is rather pale but absolutely packed with juicy, silky, spicy fruit with roundness and maturity
£7.99	9/10	Quinta de Fafide 2000	Great Douro red has youthful purply colour but grand strawberry scent and appreciable silkiness of fruit – worth the extra money

SPAIN

£4.99 9 Marisa Tempranillo Cigales 2001 *Warm, strawberry style to a light-bodied but emphatically flavoured juicy red*

£9.99 9/10 Vega Riaza Ribera del Duero 1998 *Mature dark-hearted classic has colour already browning and a wonderful almost spiritous plummy richness – epic wine for a special event*

USA

£8.99 9 West Ridge Cabernet Sauvignon 1997 *Pricey but startlingly pure Californian Cabernet of memorable, minty style*

All Marks & Spencer wines are exclusive, such as the Casa Leona wines of La Rosa estate in Chile

WHITE WINES

AUSTRALIA

£5.49	9	Coonawarra Riesling 2001	*Distinctive limey-minerally Aussie Riesling of real character*
£6.99	7	Heemskerk Sauvignon Blanc 2001	*Low-acidity Tasmanian seems rather tame, and just 11.5% alcohol*
£7.49	9	Bush View Chardonnay 2000	*Notable pure-fruit style in an oaked wine that seems elegant by Aussie standards*
£7.99	9	Twin Wells Semillon 1997	*Nice yellow colour and typical Semillon nose of banana, pineapple and whatnot, this is a lively green-fruit, light (just 10.5% alcohol) and mature dry white of unusual character*

CHILE

£5.50	9	Sierra Los Andes Chardonnay 2001	*Lemony note on top of a fresh but ripely rich flavour to an above-average Chilean*
£7.50	9	Pirque Estate Sauvignon Blanc 2001	*Successful attempt of the Everest of really lively fruit-packed Sauvignon, this works very well and finishes with brisk lime acidity*

FRANCE

£2.99	9/10	Vin de Pays du Gers 2001	*An M&S perennial that delivers good balance of zest and fleshiness, filling the mouth very well for the money*
£3.99	9/10	Sauvignon Vin de Pays du Jardin de la France 2001	*Zippy lime-topped aroma on this brisk and deliciously edgy Loire white – ranks high in an overcrowded category*
£4.49	8	Gold Label Chardonnay 2001	*Toffee-nosed Vin de Pays d'Oc has a cabbagey character some may like*

£4.99 9 Domaine du Boulas Côtes du
Rhône 2001

*Faintly pink tinge to this soft,
unctuous white CDR with a trace of
pepper and more than a trace of
alcohol at 14% – distinctive*

£4.99 9 Muscadet Le Moulin des
Cossardières 2001

*Intriguing elements in the nose of
this 'sur lie' wine and plenty of tang
in the fruit*

GERMANY

£4.99 9/10 Dükheimer Riesling 2001

*Superb straight racy Moselle tasted
as a cask sample was already
delicious*

£4.99 9 Pfalz Pinot Gris 2001

*A sort of Rhine Pinot Grigio, with
some of the smoky character of the
Italian version*

£5.49 9/10 Dükheimer Michelsberg
Riesling Kabinett 2001

*A gold-coloured extra-ripe (12%
alcohol) Moselle with tons of sweet-
apple fruit*

£7.99 9 Rauenthal Riesling,
Georg Breuer, 2000

*Very ripe (12% alcohol) with a toffee
aftertaste and complex fruit, a wine
that will keep and evolve for years*

£8.99 10 Urziger Würzgarten Riesling,
Dr Loosen, 2000

*Ambrosial nose, racy, lush Riesling
fruit, immensely satisfying wine – one
of the best Moselles to be found on
any High Street and worth the money*

ITALY

£3.99 9 Villa Masera Bianco Veronese
2001

*Soave-style wine with good colour
and fresh character – well-knit
flavour*

£4.99 9/10 Aramonte Catarratto Sicilia 2001

*Gold colour and a rich vanilla nose
suggesting an over-the-top Aussie
Chardonnay, but much more
interesting – lush Sicilian with 13.5%
alcohol*

NEW ZEALAND

£7.99 8 Shepherds Ridge Chardonnay 2000
Yellow colour, vegetal fruit and clean finish

£7.99 9/10 Shepherds Ridge Sauvignon Blanc 2001
Lovely pebbly style to this benchmark Marlborough Sauvignon at a price very competitive with big brands

PORTUGAL

£3.99 9 Quinta dos Frades Vital Chardonnay 2001
Crisp style to this Ribatejo dry white has stacks of fruit but a likeable tangy austerity

SPAIN

£3.99 9/10 Lunaran Sauvignon Rueda 2001
Nettley smell of alluring zestiness on a big, complete wine with assertive flavour right across the palate – outstanding character and value

USA

£4.99 8 Hay Station Ranch Colombard Chardonnay 2001
All-purpose Californian dry white with just 11.5% alcohol

PERSONAL NOTES:

....
....
....
....
....
....
....
....
....
....
....
....

ODDBINS

After years of uncertainty and speculation, the 230-branch Oddbins chain has finally been sold by erstwhile Canadian drinks giant Seagram. The new owner is the Castel Group, a French company best known at home for its nationwide network of Nicolas wine shops, and familiar to Londoners via the 25 branches it has in the capital.

For dedicated Oddbins customers, and there are a lot of them, what will this change of ownership signify? New boss Pierre Castel has promised the existing management in London will be allowed to keep their jobs, but has spoken of 'an extensive programme of refurbishment throughout the estate'.

So, expect the shopfitters in at your local branch soon. And as to the wines on offer, will the new French owners throw out all Oddbins' Australian, American and other long-range imports and replace them with Bordeaux and Burgundy, Muscadet and Côtes du Rhône?

Oddbins managing director Richard Macadam says no, and that the chain 'will maintain its broader range encompassing European wines, New World wines and malt whisky'.

Oddbins launched a new business with Sainsbury's in 2001 to sell wine by mail order. This curious co-operative direct-mail and internet enterprise called the Destination Wine Company has continued to advertise mixed cases for sale but the website (www.tasteforwine.co.uk) was giving an on-hold message last time I looked.

But it's the branches that matter, and given the scale of the network, you're not likely to be far from one. As chain off-licences go, they are by far the most interesting shops anywhere, with staff who are (almost) uniquely informed and attentive.

I very much hope that the new owner will not tinker too much with the successful formula. There have been rumours that the enormous range of wines will be reduced by as much as a third, but the company has denied this. The trouble is that even a chain as inspired as Oddbins has long been known to struggle to make money – it's extremely tough to compete with the supermarkets – so changes may well be on the way and it's hard to see, from a consumer's point of view, how any change could really be for the good.

Note that Oddbins' own website (**www.Oddbins.com**) is still in operation, and that in addition to the nationwide network of shops they have one in Calais, too, offering the same stock at moderately reduced prices: Oddbins Cité Europe, 139 Rue de Douvres, 62902 Coquelles Cedex. Tel 00333 21 82 07 32.

Oddbins has espoused the cause of Greek wines, and this deliciously mineral island white at £4.99 makes a good introduction

ARGENTINA

£4.99	9	Norton Barbera 2000	*Easy brambly red has juicy fruit*
£4.99	8	Norton Malbec 2001	*Distinctive but rather tough, bitter-finishing dry red*
£5.99	9	Fabre Montmayou Malbec 1998	*Rather sophisticated variation on the usual leathery theme of this grape – dense and dark, but lush*
£7.99	9	Ricardo Santos Malbec 1999	*Extravagant dense smoothie has a raisiny, dark-chocolate centre fruit – leaves a lingering impression*
£9.99	9/10	Norton Privada 1999	*Pricey wine but arguably the best Cabernet Sauvignon-based blend of Argentina – lush, complex and very special*

AUSTRALIA

£4.99	8	D'Arenberg Red Ochre 2000	*Trendy McLaren Vale Grenache-Shiraz is rather tough*
£4.99	9	Lindemans Cawarra Shiraz Cabernet 2000	*Decent spicy wine is light by Aussie standards but satisfying*
£4.99	9/10	Peter Lehmann Barossa Grenache 2001	*Very likeable super-ripe (14% alcohol) but softly squishy red has an agreeable twang of white pepper on the finish*
£4.99	8	Peter Lehmann Vine Vale Shiraz 1999	*Perennial but rather ordinary brand's chief attraction is its price*
£4.99	9	Yellow Tail Shiraz 2001	*Very dark, roasted flavours in this reasonably priced generous red (13.5% alcohol) with a fun kangaroo label and a luminous yellow polymer 'cork'*

£5.99 8 Deakin Estate Shiraz 2000   *Upfront red berry fruit, a simple glugger – and disappointingly, a pound more expensive than last year*

£5.99 8 Lindemans Bin 50 Shiraz 2000   *Good warmly spicy dense red big-brand a shade overpriced, I think*

CHILE

£3.99 10 Quiltro Cabernet Sauvignon 1999 *In June 2002, this 1999 vintage continued to be on sale after more than a year – I am amazed it hasn't sold out long ago because it's a vibrantly lively crisp Cabernet of joyous character and a great bargain*

£4.29 9 Carta Vieja Cabernet Sauvignon 2000   *Cheap and cheerful popular brand has pleasant blackcurrant fruit*

£4.99 8 Casillero del Diablo Cabernet Sauvignon 2000   *This is a top-seller in the United States – decent enough jammy red*

£4.99 9 Cono Sur Merlot 2001   *Dark purple red in the cheery cherry-fruit style – very easy to slurp*

£4.99 9 Viña Porta Cabernet Sauvignon 2000   *Reliable budget Cabernet has meatiness and grip as well as authentic blackcurranty ripeness*

£5.49 9/10 Cono Sur Pinot Noir 2001   *Great raspberry whiff off this sunny, earthy and concentrated typical Pinot with lots of grunt (14% alcohol)*

£5.99 9 Quiltro Cabernet Sauvignon Reserve 2000   *Monster (14% alcohol) dense untypical super-ripe Cabernet has plain-chocolate nose and liquorice depths*

£6.49 9 Errazuriz Cabernet Sauvignon 1999   *Gripping muscular red has 13.5% alcohol and concentrated cassis fruit – should just be at peak maturity now*

£8.99 7 Errazuriz Reserve Cabernet Sauvignon 1988   *Famous producer's top red is rather formulaic; good but not that good*

FRANCE

£3.79   7   Wild Pig 2000

Vin de Pays d'Oc has a catchy name and witty label but the wine's no great shakes

£3.99   9   Cellier L'Enclave des Papes 2001

Pseudy name doesn't mean this bargain middleweight Côte du Rhône isn't perfectly good value

£3.99   10   Mosaique Merlot 2000

Cracker of a wine, even though reading the label tends to make you dizzy – dark, warm, morello flavours, positively meaty

£3.99   9   Mosaique Syrah 2000

Good-value spicy ripe Vin de Pays d'Oc

£3.99   9   Ptomaine des Blagueurs 1997

Leafy, manageably abrasive strong Vin de Pays d'Oc improving with age

£4.29   9   Côtes du Ventoux Les Cailloux 2000

Nice warm faintly spicy Rhône red has straightforward fruit

£5.99   9/10   Château Grand Escalion 1998

Excellent value Costières de Nîmes has intensely ripe blackberry-and-vanilla fruit – a treat

£6.99   9   James Herrick Millia Passum 1998

New(ish) brand from famous Languedoc Chardonnay producer has lush Syrah fruit with weight and grip

£7.49   9/10   Château de Nages Cuvée Torres 1998

Top-of-the-heap Costières de Nîmes is muscular without being tough, and is delectably spicy

£7.49   9   Rasteau, Chapoutier, 1999

Gripping quality Rhône has years ahead of it, but is already darkly delicious

GREECE

£4.99   9   Oktana 2000

Raisiny first whiff on this suggests a very hot climate wine but it turns out to be a pleasing fruit-and-nut (in dark plain chocolate) mélange

ITALY

£4.99   8   Masi Modello delle Venezie 1999   *Light, Valpolicella-style IGT red from famed Venetian producer Masi is stylishly presented but not cheap*

NEW ZEALAND

£9.99   9   Montana Pinot Noir Reserve 1999   *New Zealand Pinot Noirs have a distinctive, eucalyptus style and density of character that makes them completely distinct from their Burgundy counterparts – this one is an excellent example and worth the high price*

PORTUGAL

£4.99   9   Bela Fonte Baga 2000   *Dark hint of coffee in this keenly berry-fruit quality red*

£6.49   9   Quinta do Crasto 2000   *Lush, new-oak red from the Douro has more than a hint of the port style about it – cool, minty and interesting*

SOUTH AFRICA

£4.99   10   Goats do Roam 2001   *Silly name-take on Côtes du Rhône but this rightly popular brand just seems to get better and better with each vintage – lush, strawberry-scented, ripe and sunny red with guts (13.5% alcohol)*

SPAIN

£4.29   9/10   Taja Jumilla 2000   *Very good value from the Alicante region, a soft but sinewy wine*

£4.99   9   Aradon Rioja 2000   *Soft-fruit unoaked red seems more like Beaujolais than Rioja – and none the worse for that*

USA

£6.49 9 Redwood Trail Pinot Noir 1998

Perennial favourite from California is brimming with sunny strawberry-raspberry aromas and flavours

£6.99 9 Fetzer Valley Oaks Cabernet Sauvignon 1998

Rich, spirity nose gives way to a gently ripe and deliciously squishy easy-drinking wine

In keeping with Oddbins' eccentric image, Quiltro from Chile (£3.99) is a brilliant cabernet labelled with mad dogs

ARGENTINA

£4.99 9/10 Norton Torrontes 2000

Soft, grapey, aromatic but nevertheless 'dry' white of real character

AUSTRALIA

£4.99 9 Wynns Coonawarra Riesling 2000

Florally scented limey-fresh mineral wine of character

£5.99 9 Lindemans Bin 65 Chardonnay 2001

Not the bargain it once was, but dependably delicious, with ripe-melon nose, lush fruit and a hint of toffee on the finish

£6.29 9 Antipodean Unoaked Chardonnay 2000

Chardonnay without the influence of oak has become a cult and the good ones have palpable purity as well as lushness – this qualifies

CHILE

£3.99 9/10 Quiltro Chardonnay 2001

Cheap and pleasingly fresh straight Chardonnay

£5.99 9 Trio Gewürztraminer 2000

Yet another good lychee-perfumed spicy-exotic aperitif wine from the grape made famous by Alsace

FRANCE

£3.99 8 Kiwi Cuvée Sauvignon Blanc 2000

Loire Valley attempt at replicating the zing and zap of New Zealand Sauvignon is only moderately successful – but cheaper here than elsewhere

£4.49 9 Sieur de Camandieu Vignier 2000

Typical peach and apricot nose on a well-priced lightweight Vin de Pays d'Oc

£4.99	9	James Herrick Chardonnay 2000	*Australian-owned Languedoc is most un-Australian in character – pale, crisp and pleasantly vegetal oak-free style*
£5.29	9/10	Pinot Blanc Cuvée Reserve, Cave de Turckheim, 2000	*Nifty Alsace has herbaceous, exotic depths and clean citrus acidity*

GERMANY

£3.99	9	Kendermann Dry Riesling 2000	*Crisp clean dry Rhine wine seems good value for money – but you wouldn't guess it was German from the bottle shape or label*
£4.99	9	Lingenfelder Bird Riesling 2001	*Pretty decent Rheinpfalz Riesling in the dry, crisp style with a very fetching label*
£7.49	9/10	Armand Riesling Kabinett, von Buhl, 1999	*Epic wine of a style more reminiscent of Australia than its Pfalz origin where it is made by top grower von Buhl – florally perfumed and crisp*

GREECE

£4.99	9/10	Boutari Santorini 2001	*Trendy and deliciously mineral island wine has dimension and genuine character, from 'one of the world's rarest grape varieties', the Assyrtiko*
£4.99	9	Gaia Notios 2000	*Oddbins specialises in Greek wines, and this fresh dry softie is a good introduction – no resemblance to Retsina*

ITALY

£3.89	10	Moscato Piemonte, Cantine Gemma, 2001	*Brilliant grapey spumante has masses of fizz, terrific freshness, honey hints and just 5.5% alcohol – amazing value*
£3.99	9	Il Padrino Grecanico-Chardonnay 2000	*Successful Sicilian blend has zest and interest*

£4.69 9/10 Trulli Chardonnay del Salento 2000

Nice complex vintage of this pineappley-exotic dry white

NEW ZEALAND

£5.99 9 Montana Unoaked Chardonnay 2000

Appetising pure-fruit chardy from NZ's biggest winery has zest and concentration

£7.99 9 Montana Reserve Marlborough Chardonnay 2000

Luxury wine has gold colour and enough rich fruit to justify the price

PORTUGAL

£4.99 9 Bela Fonte Bical 2000

Crisp but attractively complex and somehow rather old-fashioned dry white

SOUTH AFRICA

£5.99 10 Neethlingshof Gewürztraminer 2000

A Cape tilt at Alsace's most-exotic wine is a real hit – crisper than the French style, but with no sacrifice of lychee aroma and exotic spice, and competitive in price

SPAIN

£5.99 9 Cosme Palacio y Hermanos 1998

White Rioja has the vanilla creaminess of old but also the clean-acidity freshness of the new – impressive

USA

£5.99 9 Beringer Sauvignon Blanc 2001

Weight as well as zing in this bright young wine

£7.99 9 Fetzer Viognier 2000

Peachy example of this popular genre is delicious but pricier than some rivals

£8.49 10 Bonterra Chardonnay 1999

A personal favourite, this organic Californian has extraordinary purity

PERSONAL NOTES:

....
....
....
....
....
....
....
....
....
....
....
....

If you usually turn your nose up at Asti Spumante, try this Oddbins bargain – fresh, honeyed and fun and only £3.89

SAFEWAY

Although Safeway comes fourth for sheer size among the Big Five of the supermarkets, well behind Tesco, Sainsbury and Asda, I rank the chain equal first with Tesco for wine. This view has been confirmed by a tasting of more than 100 new Safeway wines this year. There seem to be so many good ones, I can safely recommend a special journey to the nearest branch.

There should be one nearby, as there are 482 in the network, not just on mainland Britain but, I am reliably informed, on Orkney, Shetland, the Isle of Wight and even Gibraltar. 'No other UK group has such wide distribution,' Safeway proudly proclaims.

Some of the larger branches have been updated in the last year or so with distinct and very much smarter licensed departments, complete with 'fine wine' sections, which offer shoppers the chance to browse among the bargains at a distance from the trolley-dodgems of the food aisles. This idea I guess might have been pinched from Waitrose, whose wine departments have always been like sanctuaries from the main scrum, but anything cribbed from Waitrose is likely to appeal to me.

Safeway, along with all the other supermarkets (including Waitrose these days) offers regular promotions based on price cuts and bin ends and these are worth investigating. You'll always get a 5 per cent discount if you buy six or more bottles of wine.

RED WINES

ARGENTINA

£3.49 8 Caballo de Plata Bonarda/ Barbera 2001 — *Italian-style sweet-bramble red is cheap and decent*

£3.99 8 Safeway Argentinian Bonarda 2001 — *Easy brambly red has a strange woody tinge in the flavour*

£4.49 8 La Nature Barbera 2000 — *Organic dry red has minty nose and some plumpness*

AUSTRALIA

£4.99 8 Jindalee Merlot 2001 — *Sweet black-cherry red with easy soft fruit and 14% alcohol – can't fault this decent commercial wine*

£4.99 8 Jindalee Shiraz 2001 — *Very dark bramble-and-pepper red for slurping (though 14% alcohol)*

£5.49 7 Tatachilla Breakneck Creek Cabernet Sauvignon 2001 — *Ten per cent pricier than last vintage and proportionally down on charm – dense colour but stalky smell and callow fruit*

£5.49 8 Eaglehawk Cabernet/Shiraz/ Merlot 1999 — *Ripe and well-put-together catch-all juicy red with modest alcohol (12.5%)*

£5.99 8 Lindemans Bin 50 Shiraz 2000 — *Good warmly spicy dense red big-brand a shade overpriced, I think*

£5.99 8 Simon Gilbert Shiraz 1999 — *Spicy blackcurrant-syrup glugger*

£7.99 9/10 Barossa Valley Estate Shiraz 2000 — *Deliciously rich-but-clean spicy smoothie by BRL Hardy confirming my view that you can get best value for money if you pay a bit above a fiver for serious Aussie wines*

£8.99 9 Haselgrove Shiraz 1999 — *Another fine spicy oaked red for special occasions*

| £9.99 | 9 | Mambre Brook Cabernet Sauvignon 1999 | *Very dark and dense Barossa Valley monster (14.5% alcohol) has all the 'mulberry and blackberry' fruit the label claims* |

BULGARIA

| £3.49 | 6 | Safeway Young Vatted Cabernet Sauvignon 2000 | *Sweet, home-winemaking-kit style of wine – maybe 2001 will be better* |

CHILE

| £4.49 | 9 | Gran Verano Carmenère 2001 | *Tannic middleweight (13.5% alcohol) has subversive charm – will probably round out with time in bottle* |

| £4.79 | 9 | Vina Morande Syrah 2000 | *Nicely 'finished' wine has seductive caramel aftertaste to follow up the softly spicy fruit* |

| £4.99 | 9 | Cono Sur Cabernet Sauvignon 1999 | *If there's still any 1999 left, grab it for the vivid blackberry fruit* |

| £4.99 | 7 | Valdivieso Malbec 2000 | *Surprisingly light example from a grape that tends to make dense, dark wine in Latin America* |

| £6.99 | 10 | Santa Rita Cabernet Sauvignon Reserva 2000 | *Chunky Cabernet (14% alcohol) with great poise and length works perfectly and fully justifies paying more than a fiver* |

| £8.99 | 9/10 | Valdivieso Single Vineyard Cabernet Franc 1999 | *Boot-black super-cassis and greenleaf nose and creamy style – a worthy successor to the 1998 and £1 cheaper* |

FRANCE

| £2.99 | 10 | Safeway Rhône Valley Red 2001 | *Brightly purple young red has eager, typically warm Rhône fruit and a refreshing quality that makes it stand well out from the crowd – highly recommended at this price* |

£3.09	8	Safeway Corbières 2001	*It was £2.99 last year, but still a decent light-middleweight for easy drinking*
£3.09	8	Safeway Minervois 2001	*Teeth-coating Languedoc red with grip and a fair amount of fruit for the money*
£3.99	9	L'Enclos des Cigales Merlot 2000	*Summer-fruit Vin de Pays d'Oc has fleshy ripeness and comforting weight*
£3.99	10	L'Enclos Domeque Syrah Malbec 2000	*Opaque purple-black colour and bright white-pepper aroma on this delicious liquorice-bottomed Languedoc red*
£3.99	9	La Nature Côtes du Luberon 2001	*Purple hue and red-berry nose on this sunny Provençal red*
£3.99	9	Safeway Cabernet Sauvignon Vin de Pays d'Oc 2000	*Worth looking out for if there's any left of the sunny 2000 vintage – perfectly ripe sunny blackcurrant fruit*
£4.99	9/10	Château Montbrun de Gautherius 2001	*Dense young Corbières with lots of spice and grip gives the impression it could improve with age*
£4.99	8	Bourgueil Les Chevaliers 2000	*Pale vigorous Loire red with strawberry-leafy smell and pleasant edgy fruit*
£4.99	9	Good Ordinary Burgundy 2000	*From the great co-operative at Buxy in the Chalonnais region, this is true southern Burgundy – pale but gripping young wine with cherry nose – tasting like Pinot Noir but actually Gamay*
£4.99	8	La Source Merlot-Syrah 2000	*Deep purple-coloured wine from famed Domaines Virginie in Languedoc has vivid concentrated fruit*

£4.99	9	Anciennes Vignes Carignan 2001	*Dark purple colour and corresponding dark aroma of blackberry, with mouthfilling fruit to match – a solid citizen of a wine*
£4.99	9	Château Villespassans, St Chinian, 2000	*Purple-black, hedgerow-fruit, gripping finish*
£4.99	8	L'If Merlot Carignan 2001	*Straight vin de pays from famed Mont Tauch co-operative (better known for Fitou)*
£4.99	9/10	Oak Aged Minervois 2000	*An upmarket edition of Safeway's consistently good value plain old Minervois, this is a blushy, purply wine with solid sunny fruit and likeably obvious oak character*
£5.49	9/10	Château Salitis, Cabardes, 1998	*Last year's note said: Maturing Languedoc red has big, ripe New World-type fruit but still lots of mouth-puckering tannin, fun to keep a couple of years to await developments – and a year on it's still on sale and coming on very nicely indeed!*
£5.99	9/10	Château Bouisset, Cuvée Eugenie La Clape, 2000	*Enticing crème de cassis richness to this dense-purple deeply concentrated Languedoc red – long, lingering flavours*
£5.99	9	Mourvèdre-Grenache, JL Denois, 1999	*Vivid raspberry fruit in a nicely rounded Vin de Pays d'Oc – good value*
£6.99	9	Vacqueyras, Domaine de la Bouscatière, 1999	*Quite pale, but this Rhône village wine is lush and sunny and notably improved on last tasting a year ago – and still a whacking 14% alcohol*

| £9.99 | 9 | Safeway Beaune 1998 | *Whiff of white pepper on alluring raspberry nose of this young-tasting burgundy – delicious firm fruit that will develop for at least a couple of years* |

HUNGARY

| £3.99 | 7 | Riverview Kekfrankos Merlot 2000 | *OK but not quite 'clean' and slightly harsh* |

ITALY

£2.99	9/10	Safeway Sicilian Red	*Perennially good value, this tangy, ripe red has a real sunny-holiday style*
£3.99	8	D'Istinto Sangiovese Merlot 2000	*Light pasta-matcher is easy drinking*
£4.49	9	La Nature Nero d'Avola 2000	*Ripe, heathery organic Sicilian with good concentration*
£4.99	10	Inycon Merlot 2000	*Monster Sicilian is densely delicious, high in alcohol at 14.5% and even higher in lingering, minty, black-cherry flavour*
£4.99	10	Albera Barbera d'Asti 2000	*Brilliant silky blackberry-fruit wine from the hills of Piedmont tastes as if it should cost a lot more*
£4.99	9	Canaletto Nero d'Avola Merlot 2000	*Big mouthful of warm spicy fruit from Sicily*

NEW ZEALAND

| £9.99 | 9 | Montana Pinot Noir Reserve 1999 | *New Zealand Pinot Noirs have a distinctive, eucalyptus style and density of character that makes them completely distinct from their Burgundy counterparts – this one is an excellent example and worth the high price* |

PORTUGAL

£3.79 4 Tamara 2001

Juicy red from Ribatejo region tasted good even though the one I tried was corky

£4.29 9 Vila Regia 1999

Made by Sogrape, a table wine from the port vineyards of the Douro, this has something of the sweet perfume of port and a lush style

£4.99 9 Bela Fonte Jaen 2000

Sweetly tarry nose on this intriguing wine from Beiras region has soft but weighty fruit

SOUTH AFRICA

£5.49 9 Stonebuck Merlot/Pinotage 1999

Earthy sort of morello-cherry soft red with well-formed mature smoothness – very likeable

£5.99 9 Lyngrove Reserve Cabernet Merlot 2000

Eager young wine with bright berry flavours – a real pleasure to drink

£6.29 6 Fairview Malbec 2000

Easy-drinking soft red doesn't warrant the price

£6.99 9 Landskroon Shiraz 2000

Lush summer fruit, glycerine and spice all figure in this dense, big-hearted wine with 13.5% alcohol

SPAIN

£3.99 9 Cruz de Piedra Garnacha 2000

Nice ripe light-middleweight from Calatayud region

£4.09 8 Don Darias

Humble blended vino de mesa of uncertain vintage and location but in its light, 'oaked-style' way – imitating Rioja, I suppose – has its charm

£4.49 9 Rene Barbier Mediterranean Red

Arty label is a lure, and the wine has genuine soft-fruit appeal

£4.99	9	Infierno 1999	*Eyecatching label on this big softie from Yecla region, and the wine for once lives up to the label – deliciously robust*
£4.99	9	Siglo 1881 2000	*Pale, orange-hued colour and roasted style speak of a very hot harvest – this is interesting stuff*
£9.99	7	Marques de Murrietta Reserva Tinto 1997	*Colour going orange and a spirity, vanilla nose on this grand Rioja, but not enough interest for the money*

USA

| £5.99 | 5 | Pepperwood Grove Syrah 1999 | *I liked this Californian wine a lot better on first tasting it a year ago – now seems unnaturally sweet* |
| £9.99 | 9 | Estancia Pinot Noir 2000 | *Super strawberry-perfumed Monterey with easy Californian charm but contemplative complexity – high price but awfully nice* |

An eye-catching label doesn't always bear fruit, but this smoothie from Safeway is a good buy at £4.99

BULGARIA

£3.79   8   **Valley of the Roses 2001**

Cabernet Sauvignon flavour in this firm (13.5% alcohol) Svischtov pink goes through from start to finish – pretty good at the price

SPAIN

£3.39   9   **El Velero Rosado 2001**

Screwcap bottle for this magenta cheapie from the Valdepeñas region doesn't detract from the crisp, grippy fresh blackcurranty fruit

Sauternes 'dessert' wines have become prohibitively expensive, so this superb half bottle is a Safeway bargain at £5.99

WHITE WINES

ARGENTINA

£4.99 9/10 La Nature Torrontes 2001

Inspired organic wine has lots of colour, Muscat-grape nose, a good spread of exotic off-dry flavours – delicious and intriguing

AUSTRALIA

£4.99 9 Eaglehawk Chardonnay 2001

Perky chardy with obvious but not overdone oak and a fresh finish – better value than the ubiquitous big-name brands

£4.99 9/10 Tatachilla Breakneck Creek Chardonnay 2001

Good helping of herbaceous fruit for your money in this plump (13.5% alcohol) oaked chardy

£5.99 9 Lindemans Bin 65 Chardonnay 2001

Not the bargain it was once, but dependably delicious, with ripe-melon nose, lush fruit and hint of toffee on the finish

£5.99 9 Yalumba Y Series Riesling 2001

Mineral, hint of lime, exciting dry wine

£6.49 9/10 Tatachilla Padthaway Chardonnay 2001

Lovely lemon-gold colour to this rich but refreshing chardy that's worth the price

£6.99 8 Annie's Lane Semillon 2001

Dry wine has nice lemony top flavour – and only 11.5% alcohol

£6.99 9 Haselgrove Sauvignon Blanc 2000

Potent asparagus nose on a well-coloured wine has corresponding asparagus flavours – lovely fresh wine that scores for sheer interest

£6.99 9 Rosemount Diamond Label Riesling 2001

Big-flavoured dry classic Aussie Riesling

£7.99 8 Alkoomi Sauvignon Blanc 2001

Nice big grassy-fresh flavour in this, but quite pricey

| £8.99 | 9 | Tatachilla Adelaide Hills Chardonnay 1999 | *Clever mix of mineral freshness and soft, agreeably custardy richness – a grand, golden wine* |

CHILE

£4.49	8	Nemesis Chardonnay Viognier 2001	*Daffy name (Nemesis being the Greek goddess of retribution) but a pleasantly inoffensive soft-fresh blend*
£4.79	9/10	Aresti Gewürztraminer 2001	*Good colour and an exotic lychee scent to this bright and spicy aperitif wine*
£4.79	9/10	35 South Sauvignon Blanc 2001	*Fresh and crisp, perhaps lacking the focus I remember from the previous vintage*
£6.49	7	Santa Rita Chardonnay Reserva 2000	*Straightforward oaked wine seems expensive*
£9.99	9	Casa Lapostolle Cuvee Alexandre Chardonnay 1999	*Pricey but deliciously opulent wine fermented in 'new' French oak Burgundy barrels' is a bargain by Burgundy standards*

FRANCE

£3.99	9	French Connection 2001	*Water white with a nettley nose, this Vaucluse vin de pays has a pleasant surprise in store – lots of zesty Sauvignon fruit and a bright finish*
£3.99	9/10	Viognier Cuvée Réserve 2000	*Generous exotic dried-fruit smell and mouthfilling off-dry fruit in this good-value Vin de Pays d'Oc*
£4.99	9	Domaine La Tour du Marechal Chardonnay 2000	*Organic Vin de Pays de l'Hérault has yellow colour, caramel-tipped nose and easy ripe fruit*
£4.99	8	Muscadet Sur Lie Cuvée Terroir la Chappelle 2000	*Not as aggressively acidic as some Muscadet and has some character*

£4.99	10	La Mouline Viognier 2000	*Fine gold colour, honeysuckle nose, a deluxe off-dry wine with perfect balance between richness and freshness*
£5.99	10	La Fleur d'Or 1999	*Fabulous Sauternes in a half bottle might look expensive, but this is cheap for such quality – lovely botrytis nose with honey notes, deliciously burnt style and poised finish*
£5.99	9	Safeway Gewürztraminer 2001	*Nice balance of freshness and exotic fruit in this Alsace wine*
£5.99	8	Via Domitia Chardonnay-Viognier Réserve Spéciale 2000	*Substantial soft oaked Vin de Pays d'Oc*
£8.99	8	Sancerre Bonnes Bouches 2000	*Pricey but deliciously lush and zesty Sauvignon from reputable producer Henri Bourgeois*
£9.99	9	Safeway Pouilly Fuissé 2000	*Flinty freshness and creamy weight combine to make a delicious, if expensive, Chardonnay*

GERMANY

£3.99	7	Langenbach St Johanner Spätlese 2000	*Soft, grapey commercial hock*
£4.49	6	Blue Nun Riesling 2000	*Brave new version of the famed brand now has more edge than the soft old version but it seems to fall between the two stools of real racy Riesling and bland Liebfraumilch – presumably in an endeavour to please everyone*
£5.99	9	St Nikolaus Wehlener Sonnenuhr Riesling Spätlese 1999	*Lush sweet-apple Moselle has apple-blossom nose, fleeting honey hint and crisp fruit*

HUNGARY

£3.29 8 Woodcutter's White 2001

Nice floral nose on this hardy perennial – a decent, soft if unsubtle dry white

£3.49 7 Safeway Hungarian Chardonnay 2001

Bracing citric dry white in the mouth despite caramelly nose – cheap, though

£3.89 7 Safeway Matra Mountain Sauvignon Blanc 2000

Good fresh gooseberry-Sauvignon nose but a bit thin and sharp

£4.29 7 Riverview Gewürztraminer 2000

Typical canned-fruit style of the exotic Gewürz grape but rather sweet

ITALY

£4.99 8 Accademia del Sole Vioca 2000

Unusual Viognier wine has buttery-scrambled-egg nose and squelchy soft off-dry fruit – mildly interesting

£4.99 9/10 Inycon Chardonnay 2001

Good new vintage of this super Sicilian has plenty of colour and appley Chardonnay character – and 13.5% alcohol

£4.99 9 Notari Frascati 2001

Breezy blossomy nose, crunchy freshness and firm flavour in this bright dry white

£5.95 9 Ca' Bianca Gavi 2000

Handsome colour, expensive creamy nose and a nice crisp top-flavour on this grand wine from Cortese grapes

£5.99 9 Trulli Premium Chardonnay 2001

Overtly grapefruit note on the nose of this extravagant but balanced oaked Chardonnay

NEW ZEALAND

£8.49 7 Grove Mill Sauvignon Blanc 2001

Gooseberries and cream in this grand wine, but rather expensive

£8.99 9 Delegats Barrique Fermented Chardonnay 1999

Extravagant oaked style with memorable lingering afterflavours

| £9.99 | 9 | Villa Maria Sauvignon Blanc Reserve 2000 | *Lashings of gooseberry fruit and a certain profundity in this top-flight Marlborough wine – nice hint of residual sweetness* |

SOUTH AFRICA

| £4.89 | 8 | Douglas Green Sauvignon Blanc 2001 | *Zingy nose, inoffensive gooseberry style with a little bit of prickliness* |
| £5.49 | 9 | Leopard's Leap Sauvignon Blanc 2001 | *Good top-edge flavour on this lively wine* |

SPAIN

£4.45	9/10	Safeway Amontillado Sherry	*Pale, pleasingly off-dry sherry by excellent Jerez firm of Emilio Lustau is a revelation – excellent wine at a low price*
£4.45	9/10	Safeway Fino Sherry	*Salty-dry and deliciously crisp sherry, also by Lustau – and just as good as big brand Tio Pepe, next door on the shelf at £8.19*
£4.99	8	Campo Viejo Barrel Fermented Viura 2000	*Surprisingly brisk for a wine with such an insouciant nose but a bit dilute*

USA

| £5.99 | 9 | Ironstone Chardonnay 2000 | *Gold colour, ripe-apple nose and big, soft insinuating oaked Chardonnay fruit – lush wine* |

ARGENTINA

£7.99　7　Chandon Argentina

'Champagne style' by the Chandon of Moët et Chandon, but it's rather shallow

ITALY

£4.99　10　Le Monferrine Asti Spumanti 1999

A spot-on marriage of gentle sweetness and sheer zest in this amazingly fresh and satisfying Asti at just 5% alcohol – great value

PERSONAL NOTES:

. . . .

. . . .

. . . .

. . . .

. . . .

. . . .

. . . .

. . . .

. . . .

. . . .

. . . .

. . . .

. . . .

. . . .

. . . .

. . . .

SAINSBURY'S

As boss of Sainsbury's drinks department, Allan Cheesman is a big cheese indeed in the wine business. Sainsbury's has accounted for about a sixth of all take-home wine sales in Britain for the last 30 years – and Cheesman has been there for nearly all of them.

But talking to him at the chain's recent tasting, you would think he's still new to the job, such is his undimmed enthusiasm. He has certainly imported and sold more wine in this country than any other individual in history, but it's the wines themselves that remain his pride and joy.

'Try this,' he says, pouring a glug of a red from the Loire, Domaine du Colombier 2001. It's a brilliantly coloured, strawberry-fruit refresher with all the classic character of its appellation, Chinon, and costs £4.99. 'It's only a relatively small producer, and we've been buying all their export wine since 1983,' he continues. 'There has been the odd disappointing year, but it's been very worthwhile maintaining the connection.'

This rather gives the lie to the notion that supermarkets buy the entire harvest of a food or drink producer for one or two years then bring ruin by suddenly terminating the relationship. Allan Cheesman is proud to have carried on many lasting contacts with wine suppliers round the world over his long tenure.

What has really changed in his time has been the creeping dominance of global brands – not just Mateus Rosé and Blue Nun but now the homogenous Australian and Californian Chardonnays and universal Cabernet Sauvignons – that now take up so much space on supermarket shelves. It does mean you have to look with more care at the range offered in a giant chain like Sainsbury's – but it's still worth the effort, because among all the anodyne dross, there are still plenty of real, individual wines to be found.

RED WINES

ARGENTINA

£3.99	9	Malambo Bonarda 2001	*Pretty good straightforward ripe dry-finishing berry-fruit style*
£4.49	9	Santa Julia Tempranillo 2001	*Dependable Santa Julia's red from the grape of Rioja is a juicy, blackcurranty glugger*
£4.99	9	Argento Malbec 2000	*Dark, dense and liquorous wine by excellent Nicolas Catena – to drink with food*
£5.99	7	Anubis Tempranillo 2001	*Strawberry whiff, simple vigorous red, rather expensive*
£6.99	10	Bright Brothers Barrica Shiraz 1999	*Top-of-the-range dark, dense and silky vanilla-toned monster (14% alcohol) has sweet lushness but nicely trimmed dry finish*
£8.99	10	Catena Cabernet Sauvignon 1999	*Strong minty dense pure-fruit style in this sublime Cabernet – really special wine*

AUSTRALIA

£3.99	9	Sainsbury's Cabernet Shiraz 2000	*Lots of proverbial upfront fruit, a distinct Cabernet style*
£4.99	9/10	Banrock Station Shiraz 2001	*Big brand, but no denying it's good – a chunky rounded spicy red much better than I remember from previous vintages*
£4.99	8	Jindalee Cabernet Sauvignon 2001	*Simple slightly woody red*
£4.99	9	Sainsbury's Petit Verdot 2001	*Likeable ripe (14% alcohol) dense red with character*
£5.49	9	Tatachilla Breakneck Creek Cabernet Sauvignon 2000	*Purple-black, red-berry fruit, soft and jolly glugger – fun wine*

£5.99	9	Lindemans Bin 45 Cabernet Sauvignon 2000	*Good black-fruit easy-drinking brand from same vintage as last year – perhaps the price hike (it used to be £4.99) has stalled sales*
£6.49	8	McWilliam's Hanwood Estate Shiraz 2000	*Dark, bramble-fruit softie is good but not cheap*
£7.99	9	Madfish Cabernet Sauvignon Merlot Cabernet Franc 2000	*Great name, and a rather elegant wine with 'soft tannins' and pure fruit – worth the money*

CHILE

£4.99	9	Cono Sur Merlot 2001	*Dark purple red in the cheery cherry-fruit style – very easy to slurp*
£4.99	9	Valdivieso Cabernet Sauvignon 2000	*Crunchy-briary fruit in this sleek quenching red*
£4.99	9	Terramater Zinfandel Shiraz 2000	*Soft-fruit style delivers beguiling mix of spice and strawberry*
£5.49	9/10	Sainsbury's Reserve Selection Cabernet Sauvignon 2000	*Straight pure blackcurrant Cabernet is delicious*
£5.49	9/10	Sainsbury's Reserve Selection Merlot 2000	*Gripping super-ripe red with lush morello fruit*
£6.49	10	Mont Gras Carmenère Reserva 1999	*Top-class mature intensely concentrated berry-ripe red has silky mouthfeel*
£6.99	8	Cono Sur Merlot Reserva 2000	*Very dark purple wine has plenty of fruit but is no bargain*
£6.99	9	Mont Gras Single Vineyard Zinfandel 2000	*Sweet seductive wholly unZin-like smoothie is hugely ripe (14% alcohol) and a real crowd-pleaser*

FRANCE

| £2.99 | 9/10 | Devereux Portan & Carignan 2001 | *Immediately likeable Vin de Pays de l'Aude has lots of young-tasting but ripe and juicy summer fruit – and seems amazingly cheap* |

£2.99	10/11	Sainsbury's Vin de Pays d'Oc Rouge	*A delicious surprise at a rock-bottom price, this has the sunniest, most comfortingly perfect sense of pure fruit ripeness*
£3.29	9	Sainsbury's Côtes de Roussillon	*Bit of a bargain, this – spicy, even peppery, non-vintage red with lots of grip*
£3.99	9/10	Sainsbury's Cuvée Prestige Côtes du Rhône 2000	*Very nice leafy-spicy CDR with completeness – a bargain*
£4.49	8	Classy Cabernet 2001	*Sunny, brambly Vin de Pays d'Oc*
£4.49	9	Domaine de Raissac Merlot 2001	*Vigorous red-berry style to a light but ripe (13.5% alcohol) Vin de Pays d'Oc*
£4.49	9	Perfect Pinot 2000	*Cleverly contrived Vin de Pays d'Oc has soft and rounded recognisable Pinot fruit*
£4.49	8	Serious Syrah 2000	*Slightly tough but nicely peppery Vin de Pays d'Oc*
£4.99	9	Côtes du Rhône Villages, Domaine Bernard, 2000	*Nicely constructed peppery-leafy wine from yet another great vintage in the Rhône*
£4.99	10	Domaine du Colombier Chinon 2001	*Delicious strawberry-fruit Loire red of terrific, distinctive character – great to see a classic wine like this in Sainsbury's*
£4.99	8	French Kiss Corbières 2001	*I'm probably prejudiced by the name in giving this 'soft, sultry' wine a lower score – quite a good oaky-smooth southern red*
£4.99	9/10	Les Jamelles Cabernet Sauvignon 2000	*Crisp, bright cassis fruit in this Vin de Pays d'Oc – very slick*
£4.99	9	Organic Syrah Vin de Pays d'Oc 2001	*Gripping young red has focused, purply fruit*

£5.99	9	Calvet Reserve 2000	*Not the fantastic wine that the 1998 vintage was, but still a very good balanced claret*
£5.99	9/10	Valréas Domaine de la Grande Bellane 1999	*Intensely ripe and spicy top-of-the-range organic Côtes du Rhône Villages*
£6.99	9/10	Hautes Côtes de Nuits Dames Huguettes 1999	*A real rarity – cheap (yes £6.99 is cheap) co-operative burgundy with the true earthy-but-slinky style of the best wines of this expensive region*
£7.99	8	Château de la Garde 1999	*Decent structured claret that could do with a bit longer in bottle*
£7.99	9	Crozes Hermitage Petite Ruche 2000	*Typical wild-berry nose and lively spicy fruit from this famous northern Rhône appellation*
£8.99	9	Réserve des Argentiers Châteauneuf-du-Pape 2000	*Nice big plump wine has two unusual qualities for Châteauneuf – it's ready to drink and not particularly overpriced*
£8.99	9	Sainsbury's Classic Selection St Emilion 1999	*This will please claret anoraks – textbook grippy claret nicely balanced between ripeness and edginess*

ITALY

£2.99	9/10	Sainsbury's Sicilia Red	*Very cheap for such a characterful aromatic and warmly spicy lightweight red*
£3.99	8	The Full Montepulciano	*Gripping sweet-centred brambly red has sufficient charm to compensate for the silly name*
£3.99	9	Sainsbury's Sangiovese di Sicilia	*Hefty Sicilian has deceptively innocent cherry nose and friendly fruit*
£3.99	9	Sainsbury's Montepulciano d'Abruzzo 2000	*Hedgerow fruit and lively vigour to this pasta-matcher*

£4.99 10/11 Inycon Syrah 2000

Dense and dark to the point of opacity, this huge (14.5% alcohol) Sicilian has massive briary fruit with a roasty, liquorice heart – terrific value

£4.99 9 Lamberti Valpolicella Classico 2001

Good concentration in this and pleasing nutskin finish

£5.99 9 A Mano Primitivo 2001

Earthy heavyweight with manageable tannin and lush fruit

£7.99 9 Sainsbury's Chianti Classico 2000

Pricey but truly 'classic' Chianti has lush dark heart to its positively elegant fruit – as good as it gets

MOROCCO

£3.99 9 Sainsbury's Moroccan Syrah 2000

Apparently the Moroccan wine industry is in mid-Renaissance: this is a Rhône-style silky-ripe and spicy midweight

PORTUGAL

£3.49 9 Ramada 2000

Whiff of clove oil and honey-minty centre to the lightweight fruit – an intriguing cheapie from Estremadura region

£3.99 9 Terra Boa 2000

Another good vintage of this keenly edged dark fruit red from Tras-Os-Montes region

£4.49 9/10 Segada Trincadeira Preta-Castelao 2000

Juicy darkly spicy and minty food wine

£5.99 9 Tinta da Anfora 1999

Smooth minty dense black-fruit wine with vanilla oakiness

SOUTH AFRICA

£5.49 9 Sainsbury's Reserve Section Pinotage 2001

This does have the inimitable Pinotage character, and as such is worth trying

| £5.49 | 8 | Sainsbury's Reserve Selection Cabernet Sauvignon Merlot 2000 | *Rather a grippy, tannic young red in the claret style that might just evolve in the bottle* |

SPAIN

£3.49	9	Don Darias	*Humble blended vino de mesa of uncertain vintage and location but in its light, 'oaked-style' way – imitating Rioja, I suppose – has its charm, especially at Sainsbury's low price*
£4.49	8	Alteza Tempranillo Cabernet Sauvignon 1999	*Pleasant squishy blackcurrant essence is an easy mouthful*
£4.49	8	Santerra Vino de Mesa 2000	*Light and somehow thoroughly Spanish holiday red*
£4.49	8	Viña Albali Tinto Reserva 1997	*Emphatically vanilla-oaked mature Valdepeñas is lightish but satisfying*
£4.99	9/10	Dama de Toro, Bodegas Fariña 1998	*Dark, chocolate-hearted smoothie has a lot of velvety appeal at this price*
£5.99	9	Enate Cabernet-Merlot 1999	*Chewy hot-climate blend from quality-producing Somontano region has ripeness and grip*

USA

| £3.99 | 9 | Sainsbury's California Ruby Cabernet | *Surprisingly tannic and well-made 'Bordeaux-style' red nothing like as horribly sweet and ersatz as expected of anything labelled 'ruby'* |
| £5.99 | 7 | Delicato Shiraz 2001 | *Dense, sweet, jammy Californian some might like* |

PINK WINES

FRANCE

£3.99	9	Big Frank's Deep Pink 2000	*Southern Vin de Pays Merlot has sunny fruit and decent grip – don't be put off by the gimmicky presentation*
£3.99	9	Cabernet Rosé Vin de Pays du Jardin de la France 2001	*Pale, salmon-steak colour and brightly fresh fruitiness*
£5.49	9/10	Cuvée Victoria Rosé de Provence 2001	*Fun-looking bottle is lived up to by sunny and lively fruit – this is about as good as rosé gets*
£5.49	9	Domaine de Sours Rosé 2001	*Posh Bordeaux pink has good blackcurrant fruit and refreshing acidity*

ITALY

£4.99	7	Inycon Cabernet Rosé 2001	*I'm a great fan of Sicily's Inycon wines, but not of this ordinary effort*

Named after the large person called Frank who makes it, this Languedoc rosé is good value at £3.99 from Sainsbury's

WHITE WINES

ARGENTINA

£3.99	9	Malambo Chenin Blanc Chardonnay 2001	*Flowery nose and likeable jumble of fruit-salad flavours*

AUSTRALIA

£4.99	9/10	Jindalee Chardonnay 2001	*Extravagant creamy-topped apple-strudel style to a fun wine at a good price*
£4.99	9	Pendulum Chardonnay 2000	*'Concept' wine in a weird silvered bottle looks a lot better in the glass – generous gold colour and rich vanilla-coconutty style*
£4.99	9	Rawsons Retreat Bin 21 2001	*Mango-nosed tropical mid-dry white from Chardonnay and Semillon has springy softness*
£6.99	9	Bridgewater Mill Sauvignon Blanc 2001	*Lively grassy limey Sauvignon bears comparison to NZ benchmark*

CHILE

£4.79	9	35 South Sauvignon Blanc 2001	*Fresh and crisp, perhaps lacking the focus I remember from the previous vintage*
£4.99	8	Cono Sur Chardonnay 2001	*Straight Chilean dry white without fault or distinction*
£4.99	9/10	Canepa Gewürztraminer 2001	*Alsace-style gem is a delicious, fresh but exotically spicy dry white with an authentic lychee whiff*

FRANCE

£2.99 8 Devereux Ugni Blanc-Chasan 2001   *Formulaic but respectable clean dry white*

£2.99 8 Sainsbury's Vin de Pays des Côtes de Gascogne   *Very cheap straight clean and light dry wine from heavy-cropping Ugni Blanc grapes (which used to go into Gascony's Armagnac brandy before the spirits slump)*

£3.79 9 Muscat de St Jean de Minervois   *Good ultra-sweet wines now rarely come as cheap as this nectarously grapey confection (half bottle)*

£3.99 8 Domaine de Pellehaut 2001   *Gascony vin de pays has a distinct grapefruit note*

£3.99 8 Réserve St Marc Sauvignon Blanc 2001   *Nice brisk first flavour on this dry Vin de Pays d'Oc, but short on crispness at end*

£3.99 8 Sauvignon Blanc Vin de Pays   *Zippy, bright and one-dimensional dry white Loire*

£3.99 7 Fruits de France Chardonnay 2001   *Appealing name, but with a low-acidity letting down all those fruits*

£3.99 6 Old Tart Terret Sauvignon Blanc 2000   *The joke really is that if it wasn't called Old Tart it would be priced at £2.99, which is about what it's really worth*

£4.49 9 Le Midi Viognier 2001   *Pretty brisk for a Viognier but the characteristic toffee and apricot is here too – nicely ripe at 13.5% alcohol*

£4.49 7 Super Sauvignon Blanc 2001   *Strange softness (is this the 'super' bit?) spoils the crispness vital to the best Sauvignons*

£4.99 9 French Revolution 2000   *From the Loire, a successful mix of soft Chenin Blanc and crisp Sauvignon Blanc – scores for refreshment value as well as interest*

£4.99	8	James Herrick Chardonnay 2000	*Australian-owned Languedoc is most un-Australian in character – pale, crisp and pleasantly vegetal oak-free style*
£4.99	9	La Baume Sauvignon Blanc 2000	*Big-brand Vin de Pays d'Oc is consistently fresh, lively and decent value*
£4.99	9	Sainsbury's Organic Chardonnay 2001	*Keenly brisk but with well-founded fruit from Languedoc*
£4.99	9/10	Vouvray la Couronne des Plantagenets 2001	*A perennial favourite, this is a really characterful honey-toned but delightfully fresh, soft demi-sec from the Loire*
£8.99	9	Sancerre La Croix Canat 2001	*Lavish and expensive authentic asparagussy Sauvignon from the famed appellation – good show-off's wine*

GERMANY

£2.29	9	Sainsbury's Liebfraumilch	*Better, fresher and livelier than branded versions at twice this price*
£3.99	9/10	Devil's Rock Riesling 2000	*Looks Australian but this racy Rhine wine is crisp, dry and definitely German*
£3.99	9/10	Kendermann Cellar Selection Dry Riesling 2000	*Clean, crisp racy wine in a Bordeaux-shape bottle is nevertheless recognisably German and none the worse for that*

ITALY

£4.29	9	Marc Xero Chardonnay	*Creamy-fruit dry style comes in a frosted bottle*
£4.99	7	Bigi Orvieto Classico 2001	*Very pale, rather straight-laced dry variation on what is occasionally an interesting theme*

| £4.99 | 8 | Connubio Pinot Grigio 2001 | *Serviceable PG has some smoky character – not bad* |
| £4.99 | 9/10 | Inycon Chardonnay 2001 | *Good new vintage of this super Sicilian has plenty of colour and appley Chardonnay character – and 13.5% alcohol* |

NEW ZEALAND

| £5.99 | 9 | Shingle Peak Pinot Gris 2001 | *Bears absolutely no resemblance to Italy's popular PG, but in its own right a deliciously aromatic exotic dry wine* |

SOUTH AFRICA

| £5.49 | 7 | Sainsbury's Reserve Selection Sauvignon Blanc 2001 | *Super tangy nose, but it is flabby – lacking the vital acidity* |
| £9.99 | 9/10 | Vergelen Reserve Sauvignon Blanc 2001 | *Lovely focused asparagus fruit, this Sauvignon from a great Cape estate really sings – pricey but up with the world's best* |

SPAIN

| £3.99 | 8 | Sainsbury's Fino Sherry | *Nice tangy nose but not as crisply dry as expected – unchallenging and cheap* |
| £3.99 | 9 | Sainsbury's Manzanilla Sherry | *Tangy on nose and in the mouth, a good example of the bone-dry style* |

USA

£3.99	8	Sainsbury's California Colombard Chardonnay	*Straight appley Chardonnay without fault*
£4.99	9	Corbett Canyon Chardonnay 2000	*Tight mineral style gives this generous wine a distinct identity among the crowd*
£8.99	8	Kendall Jackson Vintner's Reserve Chardonnay 2000	*Big brand Californian has lavish yellow colour and toffee-apple depths*

SOMERFIELD

Angela Mount is one of the big players in the British wine trade. As wine buyer for Somerfield, she is responsible for filling the shelves of more than 1,300 stores – including the Kwik Save chain – in which 13 million people throughout Britain shop every week.

With her commanding intelligence, she is at home in the role of the big-company executive. But she has an open and engaging manner and it soon becomes clear that what excites her most about her job is the distinctly down-to-earth business of seeking out the very best wines she can afford within the tough budgets imposed on the fiercely competitive world of supermarket retailing.

Angela has been at the Bristol-based company 10 years, starting just as the former 'Gateway' stores began to transmogrify into the Somerfield chain of today. And in that relatively short time she has built a range of wines that competes convincingly with the rest of the Big Five supermarkets.

But it's something of a Cinderella operation. With a turnover just short of a mere £5 billion a year Somerfield is a relatively small retailer compared to the giants, and is certainly in their shadow. But this doesn't mean for a minute that its wines aren't every bit as good. And the own-label range – accounting for about 150 of the 500 different wines it sells and entirely created by Angela Mount – is the equal of any of them. 'I want them to be the best in the business,' says Angela, 'and to be the best they have to be very good indeed.' I can vouch for these words as fair comment.

Somerfield has a website on which you can check out its latest promotions and peruse the wines in general: **www.somerfield.co.uk**.

RED WINES

ARGENTINA

£3.99 9/10 Somerfield Argentine Tempranillo 2001

This wine has moved up a gear since the last vintage – now very ripe and delicious

£4.49 10 Somerfield Argentine Sangiovese 2001

Cherry-strawberry nose, heaps of concentration and satisfying nutty finish – superb wine at this price

£4.99 9 Argento Malbec 2000

Dark, dense and liquorous wine by excellent Nicolas Catena – to drink with food

£5.29 9 Bright Bros San Juan Reserve Cabernet Sauvignon 2000

Attractive blackcurrant-and-vanilla wine has robust appeal

£6.99 10 Bright Brothers Barrica Shiraz 1999

Top-of-the-range dark, dense and silky vanilla-toned monster (14% alcohol) has sweet lushness but nicely trimmed dry finish

AUSTRALIA

£4.99 8 Jindalee Cabernet Sauvignon 2001 *Simple slightly woody red*

BULGARIA

£4.49 8 Boyar Premium Merlot 2000

Aside from the horrible lilac-coloured plastic 'cork' this wine isn't bad – middleweight cherry-style

CHILE

£4.99 9/10 Cono Sur Pinot Noir 2001

Great raspberry whiff off this sunny, earthy and concentrated typical Pinot with lots of grunt (14% alcohol)

FRANCE

£3.49 9/10 Somerfield Vin de Pays des Coteaux de l'Ardèche 2001

Yet another really convincing vintage of this ripe southern red with spice and crunch

£3.49	9	Somerfield Côtes de Roussillon 2001	*Dark and strong peppery wine at a good price from another successful Languedoc harvest*
£4.29	9	Fitou Rocher d'Ambrée 2001	*Roasted, almost raisiny, fruit at the heart of this chunky, soft centred wine*
£4.49	9	Gouts et Coleurs Syrah Mourvedre 2000	*Consistent satisfying ripe middleweight from Languedoc*
£4.99	9	Buzet Cuvée 44 1999	*New vintage of this old favourite has turned out well – grippy flavour and an aroma like a grilled red pepper*
£5.79	9	Vacqueyras 2001	*Epic Rhône red is still rather hard but packed with ripe spicy fruit*

ITALY

£2.99	9	Somerfield Sicilian Red 2000	*Good-value warm spicy lightweight*
£4.29	9	Montepulciano d'Abruzzo 2000	*Brambly, lively glugger from Aegean Italy has dense colour and refreshing properties – good cooled*
£4.49	9	Somerfield Cabernet Sauvignon delle Venezia 2000	*A perennial favourite, this unusual Italian Cabernet has pleasing abrasion over good cassis fruit*
£4.49	9	Somerfield Tuscan Red 2001	*Chianti clone at a sensible price delivers just the right cherry-fruit and nutskin finish*
£4.99	10	Inycon Merlot 2000	*Monster Sicilian is densely delicious, high in alcohol at 14.5% and even higher in lingering, minty, black-cherry flavour*

MEXICO

£4.99	9	LA Cetto Petit Sirah 1999	*Perennial rarity is a dense ripe middleweight well-matched to taco night*

PORTUGAL

£3.29   9   Ramada 2000

Whiff of clove oil and honey-minty centre to the lightweight fruit – an intriguing cheapie from Estremadura region

SOUTH AFRICA

£4.99   10   Goats do Roam 2001

Silly name-take on Côtes du Rhône but this rightly popular brand just seems to get better and better with each vintage – lush, strawberry-scented, ripe and sunny red with guts (13.5% alcohol)

£7.99   9   Spice Route Pinotage 1999

Exceptionally good burst-of-fruit wine with distinctive acidity – a shade pricey

SPAIN

£3.49   9   Don Darias

Humble blended vino de mesa of uncertain vintage and location but in its light, 'oaked-style' way – imitating Rioja, I suppose – has its charm, especially at this low price

£4.99   9   Sierra Alta Tempranillo 2000

Straight pure-fruit blackcurranty red has attractive edge

£6.99   9   Viña Cana Rioja Reserva 1996

Relishable creamy mature Rioja has good weight and satisfying strawberry fruit

ARGENTINA

£4.29 8 Somerfield Argentine
Chardonnay 2000

Medium-built ripe wine with obvious but not inelegant charm

AUSTRALIA

£4.99 9 Pendulum Chardonnay 2000

'Concept' wine in a weird silvered bottle looks a lot better in the glass – generous gold colour and rich vanilla-coconutty style

BULGARIA

£4.49 8 Boyar Premium Oak Barrel
Fermented Chardonnay 2000

Pale middleweight has less-overt oak than expected – not bad at the price

FRANCE

£4.99 8 Domaine St Agathe Chardonnay
2000

Likeable richness in this Languedoc coconut-oak wine

£4.99 8 James Herrick Chardonnay 2001

Australian-owned Languedoc is most un-Australian in character – pale, crisp and pleasantly vegetal oak-free style

£5.29 9 Domaine du Bois Viognier
Maurel Vedeau, 2000

Lush peachy Vin de Pays d'Oc is as delightful as ever, but has shot up (from £3.99) in price

£5.99 9 Gewürztraminer Caves de
Turckheim 2001

Lots of lush lychee character and a better acidity than previous years

GERMANY

£3.99 9 Devil's Rock Riesling 2001

Looks Australian but this racy Rhine wine is crisp, dry and definitely German

GREECE

£3.09 9 Samos Muscat 37.5cl

A bargain 'dessert' wine golden in colour, honeyed and grape-essence fruit and 15% alcohol

ITALY

£2.99 9 Somerfield Sicilian White — *Simple but clean dry white with a whiff of herbs*

£4.49 8 Somerfield Chardonnay delle Venezie 2001 — *Nice straightforward appley wine from Verona has a creamy note*

£4.79 9/10 Trulli Chardonnay del Salento 2000 — *Nice complex vintage of this pineappley-exotic dry white*

£4.99 9/10 Inycon Chardonnay 2001 — *Good new vintage of this super Sicilian has plenty of colour and appley Chardonnay character – and 13.5% alcohol*

£4.99 9 Marc Xero Chardonnay 2001 — *Creamy-fruit dry style comes in a frosted bottle*

NEW ZEALAND

£6.99 9/10 Oyster Bay Sauvignon Blanc 2001 — *Lively briny superfresh Marlborough classic – reasonable price*

SOUTH AFRICA

£4.29 8 Kumala Colombard Sauvignon 2000 — *Easy mix of melon-tropical fruit and fresh flavours*

£5.49 9/10 Porcupine Ridge Sauvignon Blanc 2001 — *Very lively green-fruit Sauvignon has memorable grassy freshness*

SPAIN

£3.99 9 Pergola Oaked Viura 2001 — *Likeable woody-resiny old-fashioned Rioja-style cheapie from La Mancha*

£3.99 9/10 Somerfield Fino Sherry — *A notably crisp and tangy bone-dry own-label fino for drinking cold*

TESCO

A bit like New Labour, Tesco's wine department is always brimming with initiatives. Besides the usual mantras about value for money and 'consumer choice' Tesco has in the last year espoused causes including organic wines and, rather more radically, screwcap wines.

Cork taint in wines has become such a problem that Tesco has taken a stand. 'We cannot sit back and ignore anything that reduces our customers' enjoyment of wine, or at worst puts novices off drinking wine,' says the chain's product development manager, Lindsay Talas. So Tesco has now launched a wittily named 'Unwind' screwcap range of wines which, says Lindsay, are of 'unadulterated, untainted varietal character produced from the most popular grape varieties'.

The first own-label six wines to go on the shelf are all priced at £4.99, and Tesco has made a big – and largely successful – effort to 'break down the misconception that screwcap equals cheap and nasty wine' by designing their own special bottles and labels for the purpose.

But the true test is how good the wines are. I've tasted a couple, and can report encouraging news. Tesco Unwind Merlot 2000 is a distinctly upmarket Languedoc wine, dark and smooth with a creamy background to the ripe, faintly peppery blackberry fruit – a lot of flavour and character for £4.99. Likewise for value is the Unwind Chardonnay 2001 from Australia (where else?), which has crisp freshness as well as the anticipated well-upholstered rich sweet-apple fruit. A thoroughly respectable wine. Others in the range include Italian Pinot Grigio, which Tesco claims rather forcefully is 'a far cry from the many colourless, odourless, tasteless Pinot Grigios at similar prices' and a Chilean Cabernet Sauvignon.

Tesco says these wines, which are among the total of 30-or-so screwcaps it sells, are going down very well with customers – even among those 'who shunned the idea in the past'. It sold 1.5 million bottles in the first 10 weeks of the campaign, and is now persuading suppliers that it would be a good idea to go over to screwcaps. And when Britain's biggest retailer of everything (including wine) tells its suppliers something is a good idea, those suppliers tend to agree.

Because it is such a vast network of stores – 566 at the last count – ranging from relatively dinky Metro outlets to hypermarkets bigger than football pitches, the extent of the wine range carried does vary from branch to branch. This does mean you cannot count on finding all of the wines mentioned here in every branch. But you can check whether your local store carries a particular wine by ringing the freecall central Customer Service line on 0800 505555.

Tesco also happens to have one of the best-designed websites (**www.tesco.com**). It features regularly changing offers of mixed cases, at prices reduced by as much as a third from what you would pay in store. Online shoppers should take note, but so should any wine enthusiast planning a visit to a store, because the special offers online are quite separate from those promoted in the supermarkets themselves.

An unusual aperitif (to drink chilled) at an unusually reasonable price (£5.99) this is good white port by any standard

RED WINES

ARGENTINA

£3.99 9/10 Tesco Picajuan Peak Bonarda 2000 *Soft brambly deliciously insinuating cool-fruit red is great value*

£3.99 9/10 Tesco Picajuan Peak Sangiovese 2000 *Italian-style cherry and sunshine slurper is great value*

£4.97 9 Argento Malbec 2001 *Dark, dense and liquorous wine by excellent Nicolas Catena – to drink with food*

£4.99 9/10 Santa Julia Oak-aged Merlot 2000 *Keen-edged fruit on this lively young-tasting red*

£5.99 9/10 Santa Julia Bonarda/Sangiovese Reserva 1999 *Minty nose and fruit and the cherry brightness of the Italian grape varieties make this balanced wine particularly relishable*

£8.99 9/10 Catena Cabernet Sauvignon 1996 *If you're going to push the boat out on an Argentinian wine, go for this one – sublime, silky-minty Cabernet of unforgettable style*

AUSTRALIA

£3.99 9 Casella Carramar Estate Merlot 2000 *Juicy soft young red that will chill well – cheap by Aussie standards*

£4.49 11 Miranda Rovalley Ridge Petit Verdot 2000 *Bright purply colour and a gorgeous creamy-smoky nose give way to finely balanced fruit in this hearty but elegant wine, which finishes with a delicious bite – it's been cut in price from £5.99 presumably as a bin end – so hurry!*

£6.99 9 Tesco Finest Coonawarra Cabernet Sauvignon 1997 *Deep colour is turning brown with age in this glyceriney, mouth-gripping and minty – and rather subtly delicious – Bordeaux-style Aussie red*

£6.99	9	Tesco Finest McLaren Vale Shiraz 1999	*Huge, squishy, yielding mouthful of ripe plummy fruit in this generous (14% alcohol) deep-purple smoothie*
£6.99	9/10	Wilkie Estate Organic Cabernet Merlot 2000	*So dark it's near-enough black, this Adelaide slurper has a pleasing steeped-grapeskin nose and robust summer-pudding fruit – immediately appealing and justifies the price (which is £2 down on last year)*

CHILE

£4.49	9	Santa Ines Cabernet/Merlot 2000	*Cool and minty easy-drinking middleweight has a Bordeaux nuance*
£4.99	9/10	Tesco Chilean Merlot Reserve 2000	*Bright berry top edge on the nose of this meaty (13.5% alcohol) red with a dark, liquorice heart amidst juicy-ripe fruit*
£4.99	9/10	Cono Sur Pinot Noir 2001	*Great raspberry whiff off this sunny, earthy and concentrated typical Pinot with lots of grunt (14% alcohol)*
£4.99	9	Tesco Finest Chilean Cabernet Sauvignon Reserve 2001	*Soft, upfront blackcurrant-and-vanilla formula*
£7.99	10	Cono Sur Vision Merlot Reserve 2000	*Very dense dark colour and a generous morello nose suggesting the rich, cushiony fruit beyond make this terrific – note 14% alcohol*

FRANCE

£3.99	10	Tesco Finest Corbières Reserve La Sansoure 2000	*Purple-black, jammy-nosed slurper by excellent Mont Tauch co-op in Languedoc is thrillingly mellow and juicy – and cheap*
£4.99	9	Buzet Cuvée 44 1998	*I keep coming across this brand, and keep liking it – warm and ripe with peppery hint*

£4.99	9	Tesco Finest Côtes du Rhône Villages Reserve 2000	Spearmint and spice on nose of a ripping young wine just coming into its mature prime now
£4.99	8	Tesco Finest Fitou Baron de la Tour Reserve 1999	Well-balanced, slightly tough middleweight for barbecue occasions
£4.99	9/10	Tesco Unwind Merlot 2000	Screwcap bottle for this dark and smooth wine with a creamy background to ripe, faintly peppery blackberry fruit – a lot of flavour and character for the price
£8.99	8	Perrin Vacqueyras 1998	Spicy-nosed, tannin-laden Rhône village wine is good but pricey (£1 more than last year)

GERMANY

£3.99	8	Fire Mountain Pinot Noir 1999	Pale bricky colour and ethereal nose on this unusual Rheinpfalz red, but nice crisp raspberry fruit – earthy and slight, but enjoyable

ITALY

£3.99	9	Pendulum Zinfandel 1999	Gilt-bottled Puglian plummy-raisiny winter wine
£4.99	10	Inycon Merlot 2000	Monster Sicilian is densely delicious, high in alcohol at 14.5% and even higher in lingering, minty, black-cherry flavour
£4.99	10	Inycon Syrah 2000	Dense and dark to the point of opacity, this huge (14.5% alcohol) Sicilian has massive briary fruit with a roasty, liquorice heart – terrific value

NEW ZEALAND

£5.99	9/10	Babich Cabernet Franc/ Pinotage 2000	Strange mix of South African and Bordeaux grapes makes for a raspberry-toned middleweight with the character of Burgundy

PORTUGAL

£3.49 9 Ramada 2000

Whiff of clove oil and honey-minty centre to the lightweight fruit – an intriguing cheapie from Estremadura region

£4.49 9 Bela Fonte Baga 2000

Dark hint of coffee in this keenly berry-fruit quality red

USA

£5.99 9 Tesco Finest West California Zinfandel Reserve 1999

Bright and healthy wine with warm, sunny fruit is lush and likeable

Thrillingly mellow and juicy wine at a bargain £3.99, this Corbières is among Tesco's top scorers this year

ARGENTINA

| £4.99 | 9 | Argento Chardonnay 2001 | *Lots of colour and generous well-oaked fruit – good brand value* |

AUSTRALIA

£4.49	9/10	Miranda White Pointer 2001	*Enduringly entertaining wine with shark joke, and oceans of fresh fruitiness*
£4.99	7	ICE2 Medium Chardonnay 2000	*From excellent Miranda Wines in SE Australia, this strange mélange does taste of Chardonnay and does, too, have a honey hint from the small proportion of 'noble rot' late-harvest grapes – a concocted wine for the sweet-toothed, presumably*
£4.99	9	Tesco Unwind Chardonnay 2001	*Screwcap bottle delivers a fresh, lively-creamy Chardonnay at absolutely no risk of being corked*
£5.99	10	Tesco Finest Great Southern Riesling 2001	*Very pale colour but a marvellously contrived lush-limey dry white of real interest that will repay keeping*
£5.99	8	Tesco Finest Hunter Valley Semillon 2000	*Tesco say this wine will age gracefully, but for now it is a simple fresh, crisp young dry white with the faintest honey-hint of the Semillon grape*
£5.99	9	Tesco Finest Padthaway Chardonnay 2000	*An eager wine artfully matching oaked richness with freshness – try it with roast chicken*
£6.99	9	Wilkie Estate Organic Verdelho 2000	*Well-coloured dryish white with pleasant canned-pineapple nose and butterscotch heart to the fruit – rather lush*

CHILE

£4.99 9/10 Isla Negra Chardonnay 2000

An extravagant wine with real wrap-around rich flavours, this scores especially high for exuberant freshness; Isla Negra is a brand of the leading Casablanca producer Viña Cono Sur

£4.99 9 Tesco Finest Chilean Chardonnay Reserve 2000

Made by Chile's best known producer Valdivieso, a weighty wine but so crisp it prickles the mouth at the finish

FRANCE

£2.99 8 Tesco Simply Sauvignon 2001

Vin de Pays d'Oc has an emphatically sea-grass Sauvignon nose and eager fruit – the grapefruit element stops just short of sour

£3.99 7 Château Talmont 2000

A soft-centred, low-acidity retreating dry white from the classic Sauvignon-Semillon grape blend of Bordeaux's Entre Deux Mers region

£4.49 8 Celsius Medium Chardonnay 2000

Quite a sweet Vin de Pays d'Oc and better than Liebfraumilch – from which it is presumably intended as a refuge

£4.99 9 Kiwi Cuvée Sauvignon Blanc 2001

An attempt at vin de pays level in the Loire Valley at replicating the zing and zap of New Zealand Sauvignon is much more successful than previous vintage

£5.99 8 Tesco Finest Alsace Gewürztraminer 1999

Nose positively billows with lychee aroma from this rather sweet wine by an individual grower, Rene Kuehn, rather than the usual co-operative source favoured by supermarkets

£6.99 7 Tesco Finest Chablis 2000

A nice light wine but not really expressive of the true Chablis style

| £7.99 | 9 | Tesco Finest Sancerre 2001 | *Price has gone up £1 but quality has lifted, too – a really lush grassy Sauvignon worthy of the famous appellation* |

GERMANY

£3.49	9	St Johanner Abtey Spätlese 2000	*Quite sweet, but reasonable balance – a nice and very cheap Rhine wine to drink well-chilled as an aperitif*
£3.99	9	Devil's Rock Riesling 2000	*Looks Australian but this racy Rhine wine is crisp, dry and definitely German*
£3.99	9	Kendermann Dry Riesling 2001	*Crisp clean dry Rhine wine seems good value for money – but you wouldn't guess it was German from the bottle shape or label*
£6.99	9/10	Bernkasteler Graben Riesling Kabinett 2000	*Generous, grapey, racy young Mosel Riesling in the lush but minerally-fresh sweet-apple style – a great aperitif wine, and only 8.5% alcohol*

HUNGARY

| £3.99 | 8 | Riverview Chardonnay/ Pinot Grigio 2000 | *Colour looks pink-tinged and there's plenty of mildly spicy fruit in the curious mélange* |

ITALY

| £4.99 | 6 | Lamberti Pinot Grigio 2000 | *Fresh floral nose on this big-brand promises much, but the wine is ordinary* |
| £4.99 | 9/10 | Inycon Chardonnay 2001 | *Good new vintage of this super Sicilian has plenty of colour and appley Chardonnay character – and 13.5% alcohol* |

NEW ZEALAND

£4.78 9 Nobilo White Cloud 2000

This old-fashioned wine in the medium, grapey Germanic style that once typified Kiwi whites has been getting more sophisticated in recent vintages – an easy, fresh glassful at a good price

£5.99 9 Montana Unoaked Chardonnay 2000

Appetising pure-fruit chardy from NZ's biggest winery has zest and concentration

£6.99 9 Tesco Finest Marlborough Sauvignon Blanc 2001

There's asparagus at the bottom of this greengrocery basket making for an intriguing, relatively low-acidity wine

PORTUGAL

£4.99 9 Bela Fonte Bical 2000

Crisp but attractively complex and somehow rather old-fashioned dry white

£5.99 9/10 Tesco White Port

A bargain minty, mildly spiritous (19% alcohol) aperitif port to drink chilled

PERSONAL NOTES:

....
....
....
....
....
....
....
....
....
....
....

WAITROSE

The supermarket arm of the John Lewis Partnership has become a national institution – with the one obvious drawback that it is by no means a national chain. Waitrose branches are nearly all in the southern reaches of England, with just a very few outposts north of Birmingham. They're great supermarkets, unlike any other, and I am ashamed to admit I know people from the frozen north who are prepared to make diversions on visits south just to shop in a Waitrose.

The wines and spirits in Waitrose are worth a journey in their own right. But for those who live way out of reach of a branch, this is the one feature of these supermarkets that need cause them no journey – because, for reasons unknown to me, Waitrose offers the entire range via its well-established mail-order service, Waitrose Wine Direct. And the service goes further; it offers many very grand wines that are not available through the branches, and at prices competitive with any other merchant.

Waitrose is the one supermarket capable of competing with real wine merchants. The formidable team of wine buyers, several of them Masters of Wine, seek out the real thing, and get seriously good bottles on the shelf at what are sometimes laughably low prices.

This is quality and choice in depth. At every price level, Waitrose just seems to have the best of everything. Instead of filling the shelves with big brands from Australia and California, it offers the best choice of French country and classic-region wines, the best German range of any supermarket, and the most interesting collection of wines from Italy and Spain of any supermarket. It has only a small number of own-brand wines, but what there is, is good.

Waitrose stores are rather posh, and have a reputation for being expensive. But independent consumer surveys indicate that these supermarkets are by no means any more expensive than their proletarian rivals, and this is definitely true of the wines.

In the last couple of years Waitrose has started offering regular monthly discounts on quite large numbers of its wines, and these are frequently genuine bargains.

Waitrose Wine Direct, Freepost (SW 1647), Bracknell RG12 8HX. Tel 0800 188881. Website: www.waitrose.com.

ARGENTINA

£4.49	9	Santa Julia Bonarda-Sangiovese 2001	*Cherries and blackberries in this structured, lush middleweight – very easy drinking indeed*
£4.99	9	Waitrose Malbec/Cabernet Sauvignon 2000	*Decent grippy dark wine to match a hearty meat dish*
£5.99	9/10	Anubis Malbec 2000	*Minty depths in this mature and spicy red with luxurious lingering porty fruit – splash out!*

AUSTRALIA

£3.99	9	Tea Tree Malbec/Ruby Cabernet 2001	*Leafy nose on pleasant, relatively lightweight ripe vegan-friendly red*
£4.99	9	Fisherman's Bend Cabernet Sauvignon 2000	*Over-the-top extra-ripe slurper has extravagant upfront fruit and lots of easy charm – barbecue wine*
£4.99	8	Jindalee Shiraz 2001	*Very dark bramble-and-pepper red for slurping (though 14% alcohol)*
£4.99	9	Yellow Tail Merlot 2001	*Groovy kangaroo label on this soft, squishy red – a fun wine*
£5.99	8	Angove's Stonegate Petit Verdot 2001	*Very dark and purply young wine with syrupy concentration*
£5.99	9	Yaldara Grenache Reserve 2000	*Rich porty smell on this Barossa heavyweight (14% alcohol) with sweet ripeness and glyceriney heft*
£6.99	9	Peter Lehmann Clancy's 2000	*A mix of four different grape varieties makes for a poised, Bordeaux-like (and distinctly un-Aussie) mature-tasting balanced wine*

CHILE

£3.99 9/10 San Andres Carmenère/   *Easy-going blackcurrant slurper at a*
Cabernet Sauvignon 2001   *very good price*

£4.49 9 Concha y Toro Merlot 2001   *Very dense colour, a young-tasting*
slightly syrupy style, likeable in a
gently jammy sort of way – and
much better than last year's thin
vintage

£4.99 9/10 Cono Sur Pinot Noir 2001   *Great raspberry whiff off this sunny,*
earthy and concentrated typical Pinot
with lots of grunt (14% alcohol)

£4.99 9 Santa Julia Bonarda/   *Midweight Italian-style has nice*
Sangiovese 2001   *nutty finish and bright, brisk*
fruitiness

£5.29 9 Traidcraft Carmenère 2001   *Charcoal nose, leafy-fleshy fruit –*
strongly reminiscent of a good red
Loire wine, but with more guts

£6.49 9/10 Mont Gras Carmenère   *Top-class intensely concentrated*
Reserva 2000   *berry-ripe red has silky mouthfeel*

£6.49 9 Errazuriz Cabernet   *Rather a wet-dog smell on this but a*
Sauvignon 2000   *lush strawberry-ripe Cabernet of*
insinuating character

FRANCE

£3.49 9 Les Perdrix Merlot/Cabernet   *Vaucluse vin de pays has brisk cassis*
Sauvignon 2001   *fruit, straightforward clean-tasting*
young wine

£3.59 9 Waitrose Côtes du Rhône 2000   *Rather pale and raw colour, but this*
fresh and sunny ripe young red
(13.5% alcohol) is very easy to drink,
and good value – if 2001 has
replaced it, take a chance

£3.99 9/10 Côtes du Ventoux 2001   *Well packed with juicy, peppery fruit,*
this vegan-friendly Rhône bargain
has real structure

£3.99	9	Waitrose Good Ordinary Claret 2001	*Very decent plump wine with leafy nose and a nice edgy finish – good harbinger for Bordeaux's 2001 harvest*
£3.99	7	Fortant Grenache Vin de Pays d'Oc 2001	*All-purpose sweet-woody big brand of so-so quality*
£3.99	8	Maury Vin Doux Naturel	*Raisiny mildly fortified (16.5% alcohol) ultra-sweet red wine to sip chilled with puddings or chocolate – half bottle*
£4.29	8	Saumur Les Nivières 2001	*Typical stalky Loire red is light and crisp-tasting – drink cooled*
£4.49	9	Domaine La Colombette Grenache/Syrah 2000	*Good warmly spicy crowd-pleasing red in the Côtes du Rhône style*
£4.99	8	Abbotts Ammonite Côtes du Roussillon 2000	*Briary nose and soft but solid fruit*
£5.49	9	Château Haut d'Allard 2000	*Nice pure-fruit Bordeaux with approachable ripeness*
£5.49	9	Ermitage du Pic Saint Loup 2000	*Coffee-edged solid Languedoc red*
£5.99	9	Château Pech-Latt 1999	*Good-hearted organic Corbières is robust and ripe*
£5.99	9	Côtes du Rhône, Chapoutier, 2000	*Muscular young wine from distinguished organic grower has excitingly vibrant fruit*
£6.49	9/10	Calvet Reserve 2000	*Not the fantastic wine that the 1998 vintage was, but still a very good balanced claret*
£6.49	9	La Cuvée Mythique 1998	*Upmarket Vin de Pays d'Oc has spice and grip amidst dense smoothness – fleshy but nicely edged*
£6.99	9	Saint Emilion, Yvon Mau, 2000	*Silky smoothie from a big Bordeaux producer offers good value*

| £9.99 | 9/10 | Château Beauchêne Châteauneuf du Pape 2000 | *Creamy cassis and cream whiff off this young but distinctly ready-to-drink Châteauneuf – great stuff for a special occasion* |

GREECE

| £3.89 | 9 | Pathos Xinamavro, Tsantali, 1999 | *Lively red has bright colour and keen edgy fruit – surprisingly good* |

ITALY

| £3.99 | 9 | Buonasera, Argiolas | *'Good evening' wine from Sardinia has a sweet, rustic style with a whiff of the maquis – works well* |

| £3.99 | 7 | Il Padrino Sangiovese 2000 | *Stark purple wine from Sicily is rather sweet* |

| £3.99 | 8 | Nero d'Avola/Syrah, Firriato, 2000 | *Cherry nose, earthy style from Sicily* |

| £3.99 | 9/10 | Waitrose Chianti 1999 | *Made by ubiquitous firm of Cecchi this does taste like Chianti – brisk cherry fruit, nutskin finish – and as such is very good value* |

| £4.99 | 9/10 | Albera Barbera d'Asti Superiore, 1999 | *Nice bitter finish on this perky but sleekly fruity Piedmont – loads of character* |

| £4.99 | 8 | Terra Viva Merlot del Veneto 2000 | *Organic red looks a bit raw and has a woody-stalky style but does have clean-dry fruit that will go well with food* |

| £4.99 | 9 | Vigna Alta Merlot/Cabernet, Venosa, 2000 | *Dense purply-looking stuff takes a firm grip on the tastebuds – quality food wine* |

| £7.49 | 9/10 | Chianti Classico, Rocca di Castagnoli, 1998 | *Extravagant oak-aged wine has a roasty, opulent style but still has the delicious brambly vigour of the best Chianti* |

MEXICO

£4.99 9   LA Cetto Petite Sirah 1998   *Dark, young-looking minty red*

NEW ZEALAND

£9.99 9/10 Montana Pinot Noir Reserve 1999   *New Zealand Pinot Noirs have a distinctive eucalyptus style and density of character that makes them completely distinct from their Burgundy counterparts – this one is an excellent example and worth the high price*

PORTUGAL

£4.99 9   Vinha do Monte 1999   *Typical sappy, keen-edged Portuguese style from indigenous grapes grown in Alentejo region*

£5.49 9   Altano, Symington, 1999   *From the Douro valley, home of port, this dark-purple brew is distinctly reminiscent of the fortified wine, but gently delicious and not overstrong at 12% alcohol*

£5.99 8   Manta Preta 1999   *Very dry first flavour gives way to agreeable glyceriney dark fruit*

£7.49 8   Trincadeira, JP Ramos, 1999   *Mild-mannered vanilla-oaky midweight*

£7.99 9/10 Vila Santa, JP Ramos, 1999   *Luxury red from Alentejo is young and strong (14% alcohol) with chewy, mouth-coating fruit and great charm*

ROMANIA

£3.69 8   Willow Ridge Pinot Noir/Merlot, Dealu Mare, 1999   *Simple earthy red is light in colour but firm in fruit*

SOUTH AFRICA

£3.99 9   Culemborg Cape Red 2000   *Pale-looking, maraschino-nose big brand has good balance and looks very fair value*

£4.99	10	Goats do Roam 2001	*Silly name-take on Côtes du Rhône but this rightly popular brand just seems to get better and better with each vintage – lush, strawberry-scented, ripe and sunny red with guts (13.5% alcohol)*
£5.99	9	Graham Beck Merlot 2000	*Strong syrupy but grippingly tannic morello cherry red of real character*

SPAIN

£3.49	9	Gran Lopez Tinto, Campo de Borja, 1999	*Peppery-sweet style to a mature-tasting pale-coloured wine*
£3.99	7	Totally Tinto	*Eye-catching label but not an improvement on the previous blend*
£5.89	9/10	Viña Herminia Rioja Crianza 1996	*Lovely strawberry-vanilla whiff off this bargain-priced mature Rioja with generous round fruit and grippy tannin*

USA

£6.49	7	Ironstone Vineyards Zinfandel 1998	*Strong (14% alcohol) rather anonymous Californian red*
£6.99	9	Fetzer Valley Oaks Cabernet Sauvignon 1998	*Rich, spirity nose gives way to a gently ripe and deliciously squishy easy-drinking wine*
£9.99	9/10	Bonterra Vineyards Merlot 1997	*Pricey but immensely enjoyable organic Californian has dark, ripe morello-cherry style – luscious mature subtly oaked wine for special occasions*

FRANCE

£3.99   7   Winter Hill Syrah Rosé 2000   *Mildly prickly, orange-hued Vin de Pays d'Oc*

HUNGARY

£3.49   8   Nagyrede Cabernet Sauvignon Rosé 2000   *Pale, mild-mannered pink does have some crispness, and is very cheap*

Wines from Sicily's inspired Inycon estate have amazingly consistent quality, high alcohol and near-universal availability, all at £4.99

ARGENTINA

£4.49	10	Bodega Lurton Pinot Gris 2001	*Big, soft Alsace-style to this weighty and mouthfilling exotic smoky and tangy dry white – super stuff at this price*
£4.99	9	Argento Chardonnay 2001	*Lots of colour and generous well-oaked fruit – good brand value*
£5.49	9	Cono Sur Viognier	*Dry, taut wine in a 'cold-climate' style that works well*
£6.49	9	Santa Julia Viognier Reserva 2001	*Strong, peachy, likeable caramel-centred super-ripe oaked wine*
£9.99	9/10	Catena Agrelo Vineyards Chardonnay 2000	*Powerful rich wine is as wonderful as ever but is creeping up in price*

AUSTRALIA

£3.99	8	Currawong Creek Chardonnay 2001	*Rich colour, sweet nose, appley fruit – decent Chardonnay plonk at a fair price*
£3.99	8	Tea Tree Chardonnay/ Sauvignon Blanc 2001	*Fun retro label on a so-so one-dimensional dry white*
£4.99	9/10	Jindalee Chardonnay 2001	*Extravagant creamy-topped apple-strudel style to a fun wine at a good price*
£5.99	9	Basedow Barossa Semillon 2000	*Strong emphatic dry white with pineapple fruit*
£5.99	8	Brown Bros Late Harvested Orange Muscat & Flora 2001	*Pricey but pretty good blossom-perfumed sticky*
£6.99	9/10	Charleston Pinot Gris 2001	*Smoky, exotic-fruit classic with wonderfully poised richness-dryness*
£8.99	9/10	Nepenthe Vineyards Riesling 2000	*Jolly brisk acidity on this lush limey and emphatic wine (note 14% alcohol) that leaves a big impression*

| £9.99 | 7 | Greg Norman Estates Yarra Valley Chardonnay 2000 | *Good but unremarkable brand from the winery owned by Australia's famous golfer* |

AUSTRIA

| £5.99 | 8 | Münzenrieder Beerenauslese 1999 37.5cl | *A very sweet 'dessert' wine with flavours dominated by raisins – delicious if you like that sort of thing* |

BULGARIA

| £3.99 | 8 | Blueridge Chardonnay/ Dimiat 2001 | *Exaggerated oak nose, lots of fruit, a bit short on the finish* |

CANADA

| £6.99 | 8 | Mission Hill Private Reserve Pinot Blanc 2000 | *Forest-pine whiff to this crisp but fleshy dry white from British Columbia – good but a tad pricey* |

CHILE

| £3.99 | 8 | Canepa Semillon 2000 | *All-purpose soft-dry white of indeterminate character* |

| £4.99 | 8 | Caliterra Chardonnay 2000 | *Hint of coconutty oak and fleshy-appley fruit* |

| £4.99 | 9 | 35 South Sauvignon Blanc 2001 | *Fresh and crisp, perhaps lacking the focus I remember from the previous vintage* |

| £5.49 | 9 | Carmen Vineyards Gewürztraminer 1999 | *Well-coloured, lychee-scented spicy dry wine of character – ideal with oriental food* |

ENGLAND

£3.99 9/10 Seyval Blanc Petit Fumé 1996

Nice woodsmoke whiff from this tangy, lime-finishing dry white from the New Forest

£7.25 9/10 Wickham Special Release Fumé 2000

Absolutely delicious minerally crisp-fruit dry white from Hampshire

FRANCE

£2.99 9/10 Waitrose Chardonnay 2001

Appley Loire dry wine has true Chardonnay character, and is very cheap

£3.65 9 Le Pujalet 2001

Sauvignon-style (though no Sauvignon in it) is a straight clean dry wine at a good price

£3.99 8 Bordeaux Semillon 2001

Exotically perfumed bone-dry Entre Deux Mers will appeal to purists

£3.99 9 La Cité Chardonnay 2001

Honey-wax smell and wholesome toffee-toned fruit on this relishable Vin de Pays d'Oc

£3.99 9 Waitrose Touraine Sauvignon Blanc 2001

Mouthfiller has good fruit right across the palate – satisfying as well as refreshing wine from the Loire

£4.59 9 Moulin des Groyes Sauvignon 2001

Nice nettley nose on a good straightforward focused Sauvignon

£4.79 9 Picpoul de Pinet, Château de Petit Roubié, 2001

Zesty, almost briny, style to this floral-scented Rhône curio – organically made and easy to drink

£4.99 9/10 Calvet XF Sauvignon Blanc 2001

Rare top-quality Bordeaux Sauvignon comes with grip, tang and length

£4.99 9 La Baume Viognier 2001

Typical apricot nose and peachy fruit finishing clean – at the drier end of the Viognier scale

£4.99 9 Domaine Petit Château Chardonnay 2000

Loire wine in the New World style with yellow colour and good acidity

£4.99	9	French Connection Reserve Marsanne-Roussanne 2001	*Intriguing floral Languedoc dry white*
£4.99	7	La Vieux Clos Cheverny 2001	*Fun nose of nettles and apples, but a shade too many nettles in the flavour, too*
£4.99	9	Muscat de Beaumes-de-Venise	*Mildly fortified ultra-sweet wine that tastes as if the pips have been incorporated into the flavour – fun and cheap, to be served very well chilled*
£5.99	9/10	La Baume Selection Chardonnay 1999	*Worth going the extra quid for this luxury Languedoc white in the buttery Burgundian mould*
£5.99	8	Mâcon-Villages Les Charmes, Cave de Lugny, 2001	*Characteristic spearmint whiff on this light, dry southern burgundy*
£5.99	8	Château Thieuley 2000	*Well-known Bordeaux estate's dry white has a raddishy middle fruit – very crisp and clean*
£5.99	9/10	Waitrose Alsace Gewürztraminer 1999	*High mark for this because it's fresher with less residual sugar than most current supermarket Gewürzes – but the producer is not named on the label*
£7.59	10	Château Carsin Cuvée Prestige 1998	*Honey-pineapple nose like a rich Sauternes, but this is a dry Bordeaux, with brilliant balance of lushness and freshness – exciting wine*
£8.49	7	Pouilly Fumé, Chatelain, 1999	*Fine Loire wine has alluring almondy smell and keen Sauvignon fruit but seems a shade pricey*
£8.99	9/10	Château Vignal Labrie, Monbazillac, 1997	*This honeyed 'dessert' wine has a gorgeous rich colour, an exciting perfume and flavour, and excellent clean finish – deserves attention in a realm where good examples under a tenner are rare*

| £9.99 | 9 | Fortant 'F' Limited Release Chardonnay 1998 | *Top wine from famed Fortant range of vins de pays has fine gold colour, opulent smell and handsome, minerally fruit* |

GERMANY

| £3.99 | 9 | Devil's Rock Riesling 2000 | *Looks Australian but this racy Rhine wine is crisp, dry and definitely German* |

| £3.99 | 9 | Kendermann Dry Riesling 2001 | *Crisp clean dry Rhine wine seems good value for money – but you wouldn't guess it was German from the bottle shape or label* |

| £5.99 | 9/10 | Liebfrauenstift Kirchenstück Riesling 1999 | *Lively apple-crisp Riesling with classic purity and balance* |

| £6.99 | 9/10 | Urziger Würzgarten Spätlese, Karl Erbes, 1995 | *Ghastly naff label but a lovely pale-gold Moselle with a whiff of petrol and lush fruit – and only 7% alcohol* |

| £7.99 | 9/10 | Bernkasteler Badstübe Riesling Spätlese, Dr Thanisch, 1998 | *Lovely compact racy Moselle from a great vineyard* |

HUNGARY

| £2.99 | 9 | Matra Springs 2001 | *Screwcap wine (the first ever in Waitrose?) has nice Muscat nose, soft herbaceous fruit – good value for a delicious aperitif wine* |

| £3.99 | 8 | Duna Oaked Chardonnay 2000 | *Eggy nose from oak ageing is not unpleasant on this easy quaffer* |

| £3.99 | 8 | Riverview Sauvignon Blanc 2001 | *Rather austere but very fresh* |

ITALY

| £3.99 | 9 | La Vis Pinot Grigio delle Venezie 2001 | *Soft smoky and ever-so-slightly spritzy fun dry white* |

| £3.99 | 8 | Mezzomondo Chardonnay, Valgarina, 2000 | *Wildly oaky dry white with pleasant but retreating fruit* |

£3.99	9	Zagara Catarratto Chardonnay Firriato 2000	*Lots of colour in this Sicilian with mint and toffee on nose and in fruit – formulaic but friendly*
£4.49	8	Orvieto Classico Secco, Cardeto, 2001	*Has characteristic blossomy nose and a soft acidity*
£4.99	9	Araldica Gavi 2001	*Stony style to this herbaceous and interesting Piedmont food wine*
£4.99	9/10	Inycon Chardonnay 2001	*Good new vintage of this super Sicilian has plenty of colour and appley Chardonnay character – and 13.5% alcohol*
£4.99	9	Italia Pinot Grigio 2001	*Lots of good limey acidity to finish this bright young PG*
£4.99	8	Soave Classico Vigneto Colombara, Zenato, 2001	*Cultures clash in this odd wine, and the 30% Chardonnay added comes out on top to make just another dry white, albeit a very pleasant one*
£5.49	9/10	Lugana Villa Flora, Zenato, 2001	*Rich aroma, gold colour, an elegant, complex and contemplative, long-finishing dry wine*
£5.99	8	Pinot Grigio Alto Adige, San Michele-Appiano, 2000	*Smoke and spice in this sub-Alpine lightweight*

NEW ZEALAND

£3.99	6	Tikki Ridge Dry White 2000	*Dry indeed – lots of citric acidity, a sort of Kiwi Muscadet*
£4.99	8	Azure Bay Chardonnay Semillon 2000	*Naff blue ('azure') bottle lets down a firm-fruited clean dry wine*
£4.99	9/10	Montana Riesling 2000	*Splendidly crisp-appley Riesling has creamy depths – a 'commercial' brand from NZ's biggest producer, but none the worse for that*
£5.99	10	Villa Maria Private Bin Riesling 2000	*Sweet-apple nose, a really racy, slaking limey wine of exciting style*

£6.49	10	Stoneleigh Vineyard Sauvignon Blanc 2000	*Grass, nettles, the whole wild garden on a dewy spring morning are all, no kidding, suggested by this cracking pure-fruit Marlborough masterpiece*
£6.99	9	Oyster Bay Marlborough Chardonnay 2000	*Happy mix of flinty freshness and sweet-apple lusciousness*
£7.99	9	Montana Reserve Barrique Fermented Chardonnay 1999	*Golden-coloured and opulently flavoured old-fashioned rich but balanced wine*
£7.99	9	Wither Hills Sauvignon Blanc 2000	*Fine, pure, gooseberry scented balanced wine*
£8.99	8	Craggy Range Sauvignon Blanc 2000	*Ripe style (and 13.7% alcohol) with a distinct brassica nose – pleasing but untypical*
£8.99	8	Jackson Estate Sauvignon Blanc 2000	*Subtle, intense style with green acidity*

ROMANIA

£3.49	9	Willow Ridge Sauvignon Blanc Feteasca 2000	*Gamey, vegetal nose is relishable as is tiny hint of caramel in the bottom flavour*

SOUTH AFRICA

£3.29	9	Culemborg Cape White 2000	*Very cheap and rather a good fruit-salad sort of wine with clean finish*
£3.99	8	Culemborg Unwooded Chardonnay 2001	*Clean, if a shade dilute, and refreshing*
£4.49	9	Excelsior Estate Sauvignon Blanc 2001	*Generous low-acidity faintly floral (and nectarous) crowd pleaser*
£4.99	9/10	Douglas Green Chardonnay 2001	*Brassica nose is a plus to this really relishable and structured wine with plenty of nuance*
£6.99	9	Hoopenberg Chardonnay 2000	*Worth the money – a delectable marriage of minerality and ripeness*

£6.99	8	Springfield Special Cuvée Sauvignon Blanc 2001	*Nice nettley nose, big complete super-fresh crisp wine just short of tart – a little bit pricey*
£7.99	10	Jordan Chardonnay 2000	*Outstanding butterscotch-scented pure-mineral-fruit Chardonnay of surpassing quality*
£7.99	9/10	Steenberg Sauvignon Blanc 2001	*Nose is pure asparagus, and fruit wonderfully balanced – definitely the match of Kiwi wines in this price range*

SPAIN

£4.49	9/10	Lustau Moscatel de Chipiona	*A distinctly grapey 'dessert' wine, balanced and delicious to drink as you would sherry – 15% alcohol*
£4.79	9/10	Rueda, Palacio de Bornos, 2001	*Grassy-fresh nose with gooseberry fruit – Sauvignon-style with real quality*
£4.89	9/10	Waitrose Fino Sherry	*Terrific tangy bone-dry sherry of quality equal to big brands costing nearly twice as much*
£5.99	9/10	CVNE Monopole Rioja Blanco 2000	*Splendid old-fashioned vanilla style married to zesty freshness in this well-made white Rioja*
£7.99	9	Albariño Pazo de Seoane 2001	*Herbaceous (sage in there somewhere) character to this intense and exotic dry refresher from Rias Baixas region*

USA

| £4.99 | 9 | Firestone Chardonnay 2000 | *Californian oaked wine of interest, made by heirs of the tyre company* |
| £5.99 | 8 | Fetzer Chardonnay/Viognier 2001 | *Much-advertised brand has purity and dimension* |

PERSONAL NOTES:

....
....
....
....
....
....
....
....
....
....
....
....
....
....
....

As might be expected, Waitrose's own Fino sherry is of the best kind, and good value at £4.89

A brief vocabulary

Wine labels convey a lot of information, some of it helpful. Under a combination of UK and EU regulations, the quantity and alcoholic strength of the contents must be displayed, as must the country of origin. And besides the wines from the traditional regions and appellations of France (Bordeaux, Burgundy etc.), Italy (Barolo, Chianti etc.) and Spain (Rioja, Navarra etc.) the label is also very likely to bear the name of the grape or grapes involved. In the mass market, grape names such as Chardonnay and Shiraz now count for a lot more than this or that vineyard, region or even nation.

So, this glossary includes the names of more than 60 different grape varieties along with brief descriptions of their characteristics. The varietal name on a label tells you more than anything else about what to expect of the wine.

Also in this vocabulary, which does seem to expand alarmingly in each succeeding edition of Best Wine Buys, are short summaries of the regions and appellations of recommended wines and some of the many label designations given to the style, alleged quality and regulatory classification.

Finally, I have tried to explain in simple and rational terms the many peculiar words I use in trying to convey the characteristics of wines described. 'Delicious' might need no further qualification, but the likes of 'bouncy', 'green' and 'liquorous' probably do.

abboccato – Medium-dry white wine style. Italy, especially Orvieto.

AC – see **Appellation d'Origine Contrôlée**

acidity – To be any good, every wine must have the right level of acidity. It gives wine the element of dryness or sharpness it needs to prevent cloying sweetness or dull wateriness. Too much acidity, and wine tastes raw or acetic (vinegary). Winemakers strive to create balanced acidity – either by cleverly controlling the natural processes, or by adding sugar and acid to correct imbalances.

aftertaste – The flavour that lingers in the mouth after swallowing the wine.

Aglianico – Black grape variety of southern Italy. It has romantic associations. When the ancient Greeks first colonised Italy in the 7th century BC with the prime purpose of planting it as a vineyard (the Greek name for Italy was Oenotria – land of cultivated vines), the name for the vines the Greeks brought with them was Ellenico (as in Hellas, Greece), from which Aglianico is the modern rendering. To return to the point, these ancient vines, especially in the arid volcanic landscapes of Basilicata, produce excellent dark, earthy and highly distinctive wines. A name to look out for.

Agriculture Biologique – On French wine labels, an indication that the wine has been made by organic methods.

Albariño – White grape variety of Spain makes intriguingly perfumed fresh and spicy dry wines, especially in the esteemed Rias Baixas region.

alcohol – The alcohol levels in wines are expressed in terms of alcohol by volume (abv). That is, the percentage of the volume of the wine defined as common, or ethyl, alcohol. A typical wine at 12 per cent abv is thus 12 parts alcohol and, in effect, 88 parts fruit juice.

The question of how much alcohol we can drink without harming ourselves in the short or long term is an impossible one to answer, but there is more or less general agreement among scientists that small amounts of alcohol are good for us, even if the only evidence of this is actuarial – the fact that mortality statistics show that the life expectancy of teetotallers is significantly shorter than for moderate drinkers.

According to the Department of Health, there are 'safe limits' to the amount of alcohol we should drink weekly. These limits are measured in units of alcohol, with a small glass of wine taken to be one unit. Men are advised that 28 units a week is the most they can drink without risk to health, and for women (whose liver function differs from men because of metabolic differences) the figure is 21 units.

If you wish to measure your consumption closely, note that a standard 75cl bottle of wine at 12 per cent alcohol contains 9 units. A bottle of German Moselle at 8 per cent alcohol has only 6 units, but a bottle of Australian Chardonnay at 14 per cent has 10.5.

Alentejo – Wine region of southern Portugal (immediately north of the Algarve) with a fast-improving reputation, especially for sappy, keen reds from local grape varieties including Aragones, Castelão and Trincadeira.

Almansa – DO winemaking region of Spain inland from Alicante, making great-value red wines.

Alsace – France's easternmost wine-producing region lies between the Vosges mountains and the Rhine river, with Germany beyond. These conditions make for the production of some of the world's most delicious and fascinating white wines, always sold under the name of their constituent grapes. Pinot Blanc is the most affordable – and is well worth looking out for. The 'noble' grape varieties of the region are Gewürztraminer, Muscat, Riesling and Tokay Pinot Gris and they are always made on a single-variety basis. The richest, most exotic wines are those from individual *grand cru* vineyards, which are named on the label. Some *vendange tardive* (late harvest) wines are made, but tend to be expensive. All the wines are sold in tall, slim green bottles known as *flûtes* that closely resemble those of the Mosel, and the names of producers and grape varieties are often German too, so it is widely assumed that Alsace wines are German in style, if not in nationality. But this is not the case in either particular. Alsace wines are dry and quite unique in character – and definitely French.

amontillado – see **sherry**

aperitif – If a wine is thus described, I believe it will give more pleasure before a meal than with one. Crisp, low-alcohol German wines and other delicately flavoured whites (including many dry Italians) are examples.

Appellation d'Origine Contrôlée – Commonly abbreviated to AC or AOC, it is the system under which quality wines are defined in France. About a third of the country's vast annual output qualifies, and there are more than 400 distinct AC zones. The declaration of an AC on the label signifies the wine meets standards concerning location of vineyards and wineries, grape varieties and limits on harvest per hectare, methods of cultivation and vinification, and alcohol content. Wines are inspected and tasted by state-appointed committees. The one major aspect of any given wine that an AC cannot guarantee is that you will like it – but it will certainly improve the chances.

Apulia – Anglicised name for Puglia.

Ardèche – Region of southern France to the west of the Rhône valley, home to a good vin de pays zone known as the Coteaux de l'Ardèche. Lots of decent-value reds from Syrah grapes, and some, less-interesting, dry whites.

Assyrtiko – White grape variety of Greece now commonly named on dry white wines, sometimes of great quality, from the mainland and islands.

Asti – Town and major winemaking centre in Piedmont, Italy. The sparkling (*spumante*) sweet wines made from Moscato grapes are inexpensive and often delicious. Typical alcohol level is a modest 5–7 per cent.

attack – In wine tasting, the first impression made by the wine in the mouth.

auslese – German wine-quality designation. See **QmP.**

backbone – A personal item of wine-tasting terminology. It's the impression given by a well-made wine in which the flavours are a pleasure to savour at all three stages: first sensation in the mouth; while being held in the mouth; in the aftertaste when the wine has been swallowed or spat out. Such a wine is held together by backbone.

Baga – Black grape variety indigenous to Portugal. Makes famously concentrated, juicy reds that get their deep colour from the grape's particularly thick skins. Look out for this name, now quite frequently quoted as the varietal on Portuguese wine labels. Often very good value for money.

balance – A big word in the vocabulary of wine tasting. Respectable wine must get two key things right: lots of fruitiness from the sweet grape juice, and plenty of acidity so the sweetness is 'balanced' with the crispness familiar in good dry whites and the dryness that marks out good reds. Some wines are noticeably 'well-balanced' in that they have memorable fruitiness and the clean, satisfying 'finish' (last flavour in the mouth) that ideal acidity imparts.

Barbera – Black grape variety originally of Piedmont in Italy. Most commonly seen as Barbera d'Asti, the vigorously fruity red wine made around Asti – which is better known for sweet sparkling Asti Spumante. Barbera grapes are now being grown in South America, often producing a sleeker, smoother style than at home in Italy.

Bardolino – Once-fashionable light red wine DOC of Veneto, north-west Italy. Bardolino is made principally from Corvina Veronese grapes plus Rondinella, Molinara and Negrara. Best wines are supposed to be those billed Classico, and 'superiore' is applied to those aged a year and having at least 11.5 per cent alcohol.

Barossa Valley – Famed vineyard region north of Adelaide, Australia produces hearty reds principally from Shiraz, Cabernet Sauvignon and Grenache grapes plus plenty of lush white wine from Chardonnay. Also known for limey, long-lived mineral dry whites from Riesling grapes.

barrique – Barrel in French. *En barrique* on a wine label signifies the wine has been matured in oak.

Beaujolais – Unique red wines from the southern reaches of Burgundy, France are made from Gamay grapes. Beaujolais Nouveau, the new wine of each harvest, is released on the third Thursday of every November to much ballyhoo. It provides a friendly introduction to this deliciously bouncy, fleshily fruity wine style. Decent Beaujolais for enjoying during the rest of the year has lately become rather more expensive. If splashing out, go for Beaujolais Villages, from the region's better, northern vineyards. There are ten AC zones within the northern part of the region making wines under their own names. Known as the *crus,* these are Brouilly, Chénas, Chiroubles, Côte de Brouilly, Fleurie, Juliénas, Morgon, Moulin à Vent, Regnié and St Amour and they produce most of the very best wines of the region – at prices a pound or two higher than for Beaujolais Villages.

Beaumes de Venise – Village near Châteauneuf du Pape in France's Rhône valley famous for deliciously sweet, grapey and alcoholic wine from Muscat grapes. A small number of growers also make strong (sometimes rather tough) red wines under the village name.

Beaune – One of the two winemaking centres (the other is Nuits St Georges) at the heart of Burgundy in France. Three of the region's humbler appellations take the name of the town: Côte de Beaune, Côte de Beaune-Villages and Hautes Côtes de Beaune. Wines made under these ACs are often, but by no means always, good value for money.

berry fruit – Some red wines deliver a burst of flavour in the mouth that corresponds to biting into a newly picked strawberry, blackberry or other berry fruit. So a wine described (by this writer, anyway) as having berry fruit has freshness, liveliness, immediate appeal.

bianco – White wine, Italian.

Bical – White grape variety principally of Dão region of northern Portugal. Not usually identified on labels, because most of it goes into inexpensive sparkling wines. Can make still wines of very refreshing crispness.

biodynamics – A cultivation method taking the organic approach several steps further. Biodynamic winemakers plant and tend their vineyards according to a date and time calendar 'in harmony' with the movements of the planets. Some of France's best-known wine estates subscribe, and many more are going that way. It might all sound bonkers, but it's salutary to learn that biodynamics is based on principles first described by a very eminent man, the Austrian educationist Rudolf Steiner. He's been in the news lately for having written, in 1919, that farmers crazy enough to feed animal products to cattle would drive the livestock 'mad'.

bite – In wine tasting, the impression on the palate of a wine with plenty of acidity and, often, tannin.

blanc – White wine, French.

blanc de blancs – White wine from white grapes, France. Seems to be stating the obvious, but some white wines (e.g. champagne) are made partially, or entirely, from black grapes.

blanc de noirs – White wine from black grapes, France. Usually sparkling (especially champagne) made from black Pinot Meunier and Pinot Noir grapes, with no Chardonnay or other white varieties.

blanco – White wine, Spanish and Portuguese.

Blauer Zweigelt – Black grape variety of Austria, making a large proportion of the country's red wines, some of excellent quality.

bodega – In Spain, a wine producer or wine shop.

Bonarda – Black grape variety of northern Italy. Now more widely planted in Argentina, where it makes rather elegant red wines, often representing great value.

botrytis – Full name, *botrytis cinerea,* is that of a beneficent fungus that can attack ripe grape bunches late in the season, shrivelling the berries to a gruesome-looking mess that yields concentrated juice of prized sweetness. Cheerfully known as 'noble rot', this fungus is actively encouraged by winemakers in regions as diverse as Sauternes (in Bordeaux), Monbazillac (in Bergerac), the Rhine and Mosel valleys and South Australia to make ambrosial 'dessert' wines.

bouncy – The feel in the mouth of a red wine with young, juicy fruitiness. Good Beaujolais is bouncy, as are many north-west Italian wines from Barbera and Dolcetto grapes.

Bourgogne Grand Ordinaire – Appellation of France's Burgundy region for 'ordinary' red wines from either Gamay or Pinot Noir grapes, or both. Some good-value wines, especially from the Buxy Co-operative in the southern Chalonnais area.

Bourgueil – Appellation of Loire Valley, France. Long-lived red wines from Cabernet Franc grapes.

briary – In wine tasting, associated with the flavours of fruit from prickly bushes such as blackberries.

brûlé – Pleasant burnt-toffee taste or smell, as in crème brûlée.

brut – Driest style of sparkling wine. Originally French, for very dry champagnes specially developed for the British market, but now used for sparkling wines from all round the world.

Buzet – Little-seen AC of south-west France overshadowed by Bordeaux but producing some characterful ripe reds.

Cabardès – New AC (1998) for red and rosé wines from an area of France north of Carcassonne, Aude. Principally Cabernet Sauvignon and Merlot grapes.

Cabernet Franc – Black grape variety originally of France. It makes the light-bodied and keenly-edged red wines of the Loire Valley such as Chinon and Saumur, and it is much grown in Bordeaux, especially in the appellation of St Emilion. Also now planted in Argentina, Australia and North America. Wines, especially in the Loire, are characterised by a leafy, sappy style and bold fruitiness. Most are best enjoyed young.

Cabernet Sauvignon – Black (or, rather, blue) grape variety now grown in virtually every wine-producing nation. When perfectly ripened, the grapes are smaller than many other varieties and have particularly thick skins. This means that when pressed Cabernet grapes have a high proportion of skin to juice – and that makes for wine with lots of colour and tannin (*q.v.*). In Bordeaux, the grape's traditional home, the grandest Cabernet-based wines have always been known as *vins de garde* (wines to keep) because they take years, even decades, to evolve as the effect of all that skin extraction preserves the fruit all the way to magnificent maturity. But in today's impatient world, these grapes are exploited in modern winemaking techniques to produce the sublime flavours of mature Cabernet without having to hang around for lengthy periods awaiting maturation. While there's nothing like a fine, ten-year-old claret (and nothing quite as expensive) there are many excellent Cabernets from around the world that amply illustrate this grape's characteristics. Classic smells and flavours include blackcurrants, cedar wood, chocolate, tobacco – even violets.

Cahors – An AC of the Lot Valley in south-west France once famous for 'black wine'. This was a curious concoction of straightforward wine mixed with a soupy must made by boiling up new-pressed juice to concentrate it (through evaporation) before fermentation. The myth is still perpetuated that Cahors wine continues to be made in this way, but production on this basis actually ceased 150 years ago. Cahors today is no stronger, or blacker, than the wines of neighbouring appellations.

Cairanne – Village of the appellation collectively known as the Côtes du Rhône Villages in south-east France. Cairanne is one of several villages entitled to put its name on the labels of wines made within their AC boundary, and the appearance of this name is quite reliably an indicator of a very good wine indeed.

Calatayud – DO (quality wine zone) near Zaragoza in the Aragon region of northern Spain where they're making some astonishingly good wines at bargain prices, mainly reds from Garnacha and Tempranillo grapes. These are the varieties that go into the light and oaky wines of Rioja, but in Calatayud the wines are dark, dense and decidedly different.

cantina sociale – see co-op

Carignan – Black grape variety of Mediterranean France. It is rarely identified on labels, but is a major constituent of wines from the southern Rhône and Languedoc-Roussillon regions, especially the cheaper brands. Known as Carignano in Italy and Cariñena in Spain.

Carmenère – Black grape variety once widely grown in Bordeaux but abandoned due to cultivation problems. Lately revived in South America where it is producing fine wines.

cassis – As a tasting note, signifies a wine has a noticeable blackcurrant-concentrate flavour or smell. Much associated with the Cabernet Sauvignon grape.

Castelao – Portuguese black grape variety, the same as Periquita.

Catarratto – White grape variety of Sicily. In skilled hands it can make anything from keen, green-fruit dry whites to lush, oaked super-ripe styles. Also used for marsala.

cava – The sparkling wine of Spain. Most originates in Catalonia, but the Denominacion de Origen guarantee of authenticity is open to producers in many regions of the country. Much cava is very reasonably priced even though it is made by the same method as champagne – second fermentation in bottle, known in Spain as the *metodo classico*.

CDR – Côtes du Rhône.

Cépage – Grape variety, French. 'Cépage Merlot' on a label simply means the wine is made largely or exclusively from Merlot grapes.

Chablis – Northernmost AC of France's Burgundy region. Its dry white wines from Chardonnay grapes are known for their fresh and steely style, but the best wines also age very gracefully into complex classics.

Chardonnay – The world's most-popular grape variety. Said to originate from the village of Chardonnay in the Mâconnais region of southern Burgundy, the vine is now planted in every wine-producing nation. Wines are commonly characterised by generous colour and sweet-apple smell, but styles range from lean and sharp to opulently rich. Australia started the craze for oaked Chardonnay, the gold-coloured, super-ripe, buttery upfront wines that are a caricature of lavish and outrageously expensive burgundies such as Meursault and Puligny-Montrachet. Rich to the point of egginess, these Aussie pretenders are now giving way to a sleeker, more minerally style with much less oak presence – if any at all. California and Chile, New Zealand and South Africa are competing hard to imitate the Burgundian style, and Australia's success in doing so.

Châteauneuf-du-Pape – Famed appellation centred on a picturesque village of the southern Rhône valley in France where in the 1320s the French Pope Clement V had a splendid 'new château' built for himself as a country retreat amidst his vineyards. The red wines of the AC, which can be made from 13 different grape varieties, but principally Grenache, Syrah and Mourvèdre, are regarded as the best of the southern Rhône and have become rather expensive – but they can be sensationally good. Expensive white wines are also made.

Chenin Blanc – White grape variety of the Loire Valley, France. Now also grown farther afield, especially in South Africa. Makes dry, soft white wines and also rich, sweet styles. Sadly, many low-cost Chenin wines are bland and uninteresting.

cherry – In wine-tasting, either a pale red colour or, more commonly, a smell or flavour akin to the sun-warmed, bursting sweet ripeness of cherries. Many Italian wines, from lightweights such as Bardolino and Valpolicella to serious Chianti, have this character. 'Black cherry' as a description is often used of Merlot wines – meaning they are sweet but have a firmness associated with the thicker skins of black cherries.

Cinsault – Black grape variety of southern France, where it is invariably blended with others in wines of all qualities ranging from vins de pays to the pricey reds of Châteauneuf du Pape. Also much planted in South Africa. The effect in wine is to add keen aromas (sometimes compared with turpentine!) and softness to the blend. The name is often spelt Cinsaut.

Clape, La – A small *cru* (*q.v.*) within the Coteaux du Languedoc where the growers make some seriously delicious red wines, mainly from Carignan, Grenache and Syrah grapes. A name worth looking out for on labels from the region.

claret – The red wine of Bordeaux, France. It comes from Latin *clarus,* meaning clear, recalling a time when the red wines of the region were much lighter in colour than they are now.

clarete – On Spanish and Portuguese labels indicates a pale-coloured red wine. *Tinto* signifies a deeper hue.

classic – An overused term in every respect – wine descriptions being no exception. In this book, the word is used to describe a very good wine of its type. So, a 'classic' Cabernet Sauvignon is one that is recognisably and admirably characteristic of that grape.

Classico – Under Italy's wine laws, this word appended to the name of a DOC zone has an important significance. The Classico wines of the region can be made only from vineyards lying in the best-rated areas, and wines thus labelled (e.g. Chianti Classico, Soave Classico, Valpolicella Classico) can reliably be counted on to be a cut above the rest.

Colombard – White grape variety of southern France. Once employed almost entirely for making the wine that is distilled for Armagnac and Cognac brandies, but lately restored to varietal prominence in the Vin de Pays des Côtes de Gascogne where hi-tech wineries turn it into a fresh and crisp, if unchallenging, dry wine at a budget price. But beware – cheap Colombard (especially from South Africa) can still be very dull.

concept wines – A marketing term now very much part of the wine vocabulary. More and more wines are labelled with names portraying a concept rather than indicating the nature of the wine itself. Examples include Tesco's 'Unwindy' range of wines with screwcap closures.

co-op – Very many of France's good-quality, inexpensive wines are made by co-operatives. These are wine-producing factories whose members, and joint-owners, are local *vignerons* (vine-growers). Each year they sell their harvests to the co-op for turning into branded wines. In Italy, co-op wines can be identified by the words *Cantina Sociale* on the label and in Germany by the term *Winzergenossenschaft.*

Corbières – A name to look out for. It's an AC of France's Midi (deep south) and produces countless robust reds and a few interesting whites, often at bargain prices.

Cortese – Obscure white grape variety of Piedmont, Italy. At its best, makes amazingly delicious, keenly brisk and fascinating wines. Worth seeking out.

Costières de Nîmes – An AC of Languedoc-Roussillon in southern France. It's a name to look out for, the best red wines being notable for their concentration of colour and fruit, with the earthy-spiciness of the better Rhône wines and a likeable liquorice note. Good white wines, too, and even a decent rosé or two.

côte – In French, it simply means a side, or slope, of a hill. The implication in wine terms is that the grapes come from a vineyard ideally situated for maximum sunlight, good drainage and the unique soil conditions prevailing on the hill in question. It's fair enough to claim that vines grown on slopes might get more sunlight than those grown on the flat, but there is no guarantee whatsoever that any wine labelled 'Côtes du' this or that is made from grapes grown on a hillside anyway. Côtes du Rhône wines are a case in point. Many 'côtes' wines come from entirely level vineyards and it is worth remembering that many of the vineyards of Bordeaux, producing most of the world's priciest wines, are little short of prairie flat. The quality factor is determined much more significantly by the weather and the talents of the winemaker.

Côtes du Luberon – Appellation Contrôlée zone of Provence in south-east France. Wines, mostly red, are similar in style to Côtes du Rhône.

Côtes du Rhône – One of the biggest and best-known appellations of south-east France, covering an area roughly defined by the southern reaches of the Rhône valley. Long notorious for cheap and execrable reds, the Côtes du Rhône AC has lately achieved remarkable improvements in quality at all points along the price scale. Lots of brilliant-value warm and spicy reds, principally from Grenache and Syrah grapes. There are some white and rosé wines.

Côtes du Rhône Villages – Appellation within the larger Côtes du Rhône AC for wine of supposed superiority made in a number of zones associated with a long list of nominated individual villages. Villages wines can be more interesting than their humbler counterparts, but this cannot be counted on.

Côtes du Roussillon – Huge appellation of south-west France known for strong, dark, peppery reds often offering very decent value.

Côtes du Roussillon Villages – Appellation for superior wines from a number of nominated locations within the larger Roussillon AC. Some of these village wines can be of exceptional quality and value.

crianza – Means 'nursery' in Spanish. On Rioja and Navarra wines, the designation signifies a wine that has been nursed through a maturing period of at least a year in oak casks and a further six months in bottle before being released for sale.

cru – A word that crops up with confusing regularity on French wine labels. It means 'the growing' or 'the making' of a wine and asserts that the wine concerned is from a specific vineyard. Under the Appellation Contrôlée rules, countless *crus* are classified in various hierarchical ranks. Hundreds of individual vineyards are described as *premier cru* or *grand cru* in the classic wine regions of Alsace, Bordeaux, Burgundy and Champagne. The common denominator in all these is that the wine can be counted on to be enormously expensive. On humbler wines, the use of the word 'cru' tends to be mere decoration.

cuve – A vat for wine, French.

cuvée – French for the wine in a *cuve* or vat. The word is much used on labels to imply that the wine is from just one vat, and thus of unique, unblended character. *Premier cuvée* is supposedly the best wine from a given pressing because the grapes have had only the initial, gentle squashing to extract the free-run juice. Subsequent *cuvées* will have been from harsher pressings, grinding the grape pulp to extract the last drop of juice.

Dão – Major wine-producing region of northern Portugal now producing much more interesting reds than it used to. It's worth looking out for anything made by mega-producer Sogrape.

demi sec – 'Half-dry' style of French (and some other) wines. Beware – it can mean anything from off-dry to cloyingly sweet.

DO – Denominacion de Origen, Spain's wine-regulating scheme, similar to France's AC, but older – the first DO region was Rioja, from 1926. DO wines are Spain's best, accounting for a third of the annual crop.

DOC – Denominazione di Origine Controllata, Italy's equivalent of France's AC. The wines are made according to the stipulations of each of its 280 denominated zones of origin, 20 of which enjoy the superior classification of DOCG (DOC with Garantita appended).

Durif – Rare black grape variety mostly of California, where it is also known as Petite Sirah, but with some plantings in Australia.

earthy – A tricky word in the wine vocabulary. In this book, its use is meant to be complimentary. It indicates that the wine somehow suggests the soil the grapes were grown in, even (perhaps a shade too poetically) the landscape in which the vineyards lie. The amazing-value red wines of the torrid, volcanic southernmost regions of Italy are often described as earthy. This is an association with the pleasantly 'scorched' back-flavour in wines made from the ultra-ripe harvests of this near-sub-tropical part of the world.

edge – A wine with edge is one with evident (not excessive) acidity.

élevé – Raised, in the sense of 'brought up', in French. Much used on wine labels where the wine has been matured in oak barrels *(élevé en fûts de chêne)* to give it extra dimensions.

Entre Deux Mers – Meaning 'between two seas', it's a region lying between the Dordogne and Garonne rivers of Bordeaux, now mainly known for dry white wines from Sauvignon and Semillon grapes. Quality is rarely exciting.

Estremadura – Wine-producing region occupying Portugal's coastal area north of Lisbon. Lots of interesting wines from indigenous grape varieties, usually at bargain prices. If a label mentions Estremadura, it is a safe bet that there might be something good within.

Faugères – AC of the Languedoc in south-west France. Source of many hearty, economic reds.

Feteasca – White grape variety widely grown in Romania. Name means 'maiden's grape' and the wine tends to be soft and slightly sweet.

finish – The last flavour lingering in the mouth after wine has been swallowed.

fino – Pale and very dry style of sherry. You drink it thoroughly chilled – and you don't keep it any longer after opening than other dry white wine. Needs to be fresh to be at its best.

Fitou – One of the first 'designer' wines, it's an appellation in France's Languedoc region, where production is dominated by one huge co-operative, the Vignerons de Mont Tauch. Back in the 1970s, this co-op paid a corporate-image company to come up with a Fitou logo and label-design style, and the wines have prospered ever since. And it's not just packaging – Fitou at all price levels can be very good value, especially from the Mont Tauch co-op.

flabby – Fun word describing a wine that tastes dilute or watery, with insufficient acidity.

flying winemaker – Back-labels on supermarket wines used to boast that the contents were made by a flying winemaker. Nowadays, the use of these consultants is less overt, but they continue to visit vineyards worldwide at harvest time to oversee the production process, perhaps to ensure that the style of wine wanted by a major customer (usually a supermarket) is adhered to by the locals. These people are very often Australian, with degrees in oenology (the science of winemaking) and well up on the latest technology and biochemistry. If there is a criticism of flying winemakers it is that they have a tendency to impose a uniform style on all the vineyards upon which they descend. Thus, more and more French, Italian and Spanish wines, for example, are starting to take on the 'upfront fruitiness' of the wines of Australia.

frizzante – see *spumante*

fruit – In tasting terms, the fruit is the greater part of the overall flavour of a wine. After all, the wine is (or should be) composed entirely of fruit.

Gamay – The black grape that makes all red Beaujolais. It is a pretty safe rule to avoid Gamay wines from any other region as the grape does not do well elsewhere.

Garganega – White grape variety of the Veneto region of north-west Italy. Best known as the principal ingredient of Soave, but occasionally included in varietal blends and mentioned as such on labels.

Garnacha – Spanish black grape variety synonymous with Grenache of France. It is blended with Tempranillo to make the red wines of Rioja and Navarra, and is now quite widely cultivated elsewhere in Spain to make grippingly fruity varietals.

Gavi – DOC for dry but rich white wine from Cortese grapes in Piedmont, north-east Italy. Trendy Gavi di Gavi wines tend to be enjoyably lush, but are rather expensive.

Gewürztraminer – One of the great grape varieties of Alsace, France. At their best, the wines are perfumed with lychees and are richly, spicily fruity, yet quite dry. Gewürztraminer from Alsace is almost always expensive – never under £5 – but the grape is also grown with some success in Eastern Europe, Germany, Italy and South America, and sold at more approachable prices. Pronounced 'geh VOORTS tram eener'.

Graciano – Black grape variety of Spain is one of the minor constituents of Rioja. Better known in its own right in Australia where it can make dense, spicy long-lived red wines.

green – In flavour, a wine that is unripe and raw-tasting.

Grenache – The mainstay of the wines of the southern Rhône Valley in France. Grenache is usually the greater part of the mix in Côtes du Rhône reds and is widely planted right across the neighbouring Languedoc-Roussillon region. It's a big-cropping variety that thrives even in the hottest climates and is really a blending grape – most commonly with Syrah, the noble variety of the northern Rhône. Few French wines are labelled with its name, but the grape has caught on in Australia in a big way and it is now becoming a familiar varietal, known for strong, dark liquorous reds. Grenache is the French name for what was originally a Spanish variety, Garnacha.

grip – In wine-tasting terminology, the sensation in the mouth produced by a wine that has a healthy quantity of tannin in it. A wine with grip is a good wine. A wine with too much tannin, or which is still too young (the tannin hasn't 'softened' with age) is not described as having grip, but as mouth-puckering – or simply undrinkable.

Grüner Veltliner – The 'national' white-wine grape of Austria. In the past it made mostly soft, German-style everyday wines, but now is behind some excellent dry styles, too.

halbtrocken – 'Half-dry' in Germany's wine vocabulary. A reassurance that the wine is not some ghastly sugared Liebfraumilch-style confection.

hock – The wine of Germany's Rhine river valleys. It comes in brown bottles, as distinct from the wine of the Mosel river valleys – which comes in green ones.

IGT – Indicazione Geografica Tipica. Italy's recently instituted wine-quality designation, broadly equivalent to France's vin de pays. The label has to state the geographical location of the vineyard and will often (but not always) state the principal grape varieties from which the wine is made.

Inycon – A wine brand of Sicily's huge Settesoli co-operative and the label on several of the highest-rated wines in this book. Inycon was the Ancient Greek name of the modern Sicilian village of Menfi where the vineyards and winery for this remarkable brand have been established.

jammy – The 'sweetness' in dry red wines is supposed to evoke ripeness rather than sugariness. Sometimes flavours include a sweetness reminiscent of jam. Usually a fault in the winemaking technique.

joven – Young wine, Spanish. In regions such as Rioja, *vino joven* is a synonym for *sin crianza*, 'without ageing' in cask or bottle.

Kabinett – Under Germany's bewildering wine-quality rules, this is a classification of a top-quality (QmP – *q.v.*) wine. Expect a keen, dry, racy style. The name comes from the cabinet or cupboard in which winemakers traditionally kept their most treasured bottles.

Kekfrankos – Black grape variety of Hungary, particularly the Sopron region, which makes some of the country's more interesting red wines, characterised by colour and spiciness. Same variety as Austria's Blaufrankisch.

Lambrusco – The name is that of a black grape variety widely grown across northern Italy. True Lambrusco wine is red, dry and very slightly sparkling but from the 1980s Britain has been deluged with a strange, sweet manifestation of the style that has done little to enhance the good name of the original. Good Lambrusco is delicious and fun.

Languedoc-Roussillon – Vast area of southern France, including the country's south-west Mediterranean region. The source, now, of many great-value wines from countless ACs and vin de pays zones.

legs – The colourless alcohol in the wine left clinging to the inside of the glass after the contents have been swirled. The persistence of the legs is an indicator of the concentration of the alcohol. Also known as 'tears'.

liquorice – The pungent, slightly burnt flavours of this once-fashionable confection are detectable in some wines made from very ripe grapes, for example the Malbec harvested in Argentina and several varieties grown in the very hot vineyards of southernmost Italy. A close synonym is 'tarry'. This characteristic is by no means a fault in red wine, unless very dominant, but it can make for a challenging flavour that might not appeal to all tastes.

liquorous – Wines of great weight and glyceriney texture – evidenced by their 'legs' (*q.v.*) – are always noteworthy. The connection with liquor is drawn in respect of the feel of the wine in the mouth, rather than with the higher alcoholic strength of spirits.

Lugana – DOC of Lombardy, Italy known for a dry white wine that is often of real distinction – rich, almondy stuff from the ubiquitous Trebbiano grape.

Macabeo – One of the main grapes used for cava, the sparkling wine of Spain. It is the same grape as Viura.

Mâcon – Town and collective appellation of southern Burgundy, France. Lightweight white wines from Chardonnay grapes and similarly light reds from Pinot Noir and some Gamay. The better ones, and the ones exported, have the AC Mâcon-Villages and there are individual-village wines with their own ACs including Mâcon-Clessé, Mâcon-Viré and Mâcon-Lugny.

Malbec – Black grape variety grown on a small scale in Bordeaux, and the mainstay of the wines of Cahors in France's Dordogne region under the name Cot. Now much better known for producing big butch reds in Argentina.

Mantinia – Winemaking region of the Peloponnese, Greece. Dry whites from Moschofilero grapes are aromatic and refreshing.

Manzanilla – Pale, very dry sherry of Sanlucar de Barrameida, a grungy seaport on the southernmost coast of Spain. Manzanilla is proud to be distinct from the pale, very dry fino sherry of the main producing town of Jerez de la Frontera down the coast. Drink it chilled and fresh – it goes downhill in an opened bottle after just a few days, even if kept (as it should be) in the fridge.

Margaret River – Vineyard region of Western Australia regarded as ideal for grape varieties including Cabernet Sauvignon. It has a relatively cool climate and a reputation for making sophisticated wines, both red and white.

Marlborough – Best-known vineyard region of New Zealand's South Island has a cool climate and a name for brisk but cerebral Sauvignon and Chardonnay wines.

Marsanne – White grape variety of the northern Rhône Valley and, increasingly, of the wider south of France. It's known for making well-coloured wines with heady aroma and fruit.

Mataro – Black grape variety of Australia. It's the same as the Mourvèdre of France.

McLaren Vale – Vineyard region south of Adelaide in SE Australia. Known for serious-quality wines from grape varieties including Shiraz and Chardonnay.

meaty – Weighty, rich red wine style.

Mendoza – The region to watch in Argentina. Lying to the east of the Andes mountains, just about opposite the best vineyards of Chile on the other side, Mendoza accounts for the bulk of Argentine wine production, with quality improving fast.

Merlot – One of the great black wine grapes of Bordeaux, and now grown all over the world. The name is said to derive from the French *merle*, a blackbird. Characteristics of Merlot-based wines attract descriptions such as 'plummy' and 'plump' with black-cherry aroma. The grapes are larger than most, and thus have less skin in proportion to their flesh. This means the resulting wines have less tannin than wines from smaller-berry varieties such as Cabernet Sauvignon, and are therefore, in the Bordeaux context at least, more suitable for drinking while still relatively young.

middle palate – In wine-tasting, the impression given by the wine when it is held in the mouth.

Midi – Catch-all term for the deep south of France west of the Rhône Valley.

mineral – Good dry white wines can have a crispness and freshness that somehow evokes this word. Purity of flavour is a key.

Minervois – AC for (mostly) red wines from vineyards around the town of Minerve in the Languedoc-Roussillon region of France. Often good value.

Monastrell – Black grape variety of Spain, widely planted in Mediterranean regions for inexpensive wines notable for their high alcohol and toughness – though they can mature into excellent, soft reds. The variety is known in France as Mourvèdre and in Australia as Mataro.

Monbazillac – AC for sweet 'dessert' wines within the wider appellation of Bergerac in south-west France. Made from the same grape varieties (principally Sauvignon and Semillon) that go into the much costlier counterpart wines of Barsac and Sauternes near Bordeaux, these stickies from botrytis-affected, late-harvested grapes can be delicious and good value for money.

Montalcino – Hilltown of Tuscany, Italy, and a DOCG for strong and very long-lived red wines from Brunello grapes. The wines are mostly very expensive. Rosso di Montalcino, a DOC for the humbler wines of the zone, is often a good buy.

Montepulciano – Black grape variety of Italy. Best-known in Montepulciano d'Abruzzo, the juicy, purply-black and bramble-fruited red of the Abruzzi region mid-way down Italy's Adriatic side. Also the grape in the rightly popular hearty reds of Rosso Conero from around Ancona in the Marches. Not to be confused with the hilltown of Montepulciano in Tuscany, famous for expensive Vino Nobile di Montepulciano wine.

morello – Lots of red wines have smells and flavours redolent of cherries. Morello cherries, among the darkest-coloured and sweetest of all varieties and the preferred choice of cherry brandy producers, have a distinct sweetness resembling some wines made from Merlot grapes. A morello whiff or taste is generally very welcome.

Moscatel – Spanish Muscat.

Moscato – see **Muscat**

Moselle – The wine of Germany's Mosel river valleys, collectively known for winemaking purposes as Mosel-Saar-Ruwer. The wine always comes in slim, green bottles, as distinct from the brown bottles employed for Rhine wines.

Mourvèdre – Widely planted black grape variety of southern France. It's an ingredient in many of the wines of Provence, the Rhône and Languedoc, including the ubiquitous Vin de Pays d'Oc. It's a hot-climate vine and the wine is usually blended with other varieties to give sweet aromas and 'backbone' to the mix. Known as Mataro in Australia and Monastrell in Spain.

Muscadet – One of France's best-known everyday whites. It comes from vineyards at the estuarial end of the river Loire, and at its best has something of a sea-breezy freshness about it. The better wines are reckoned to be those from the vineyards in the Sèvre et Maine region, and many are made *sur lie* – 'on the lees' – meaning that the wine is left in contact with the yeasty deposit of its fermentation until just before bottling, in an endeavour to add interest to what can sometimes be an acidic and fruitless style.

Muscat – Grape variety with origins in ancient Greece, and still grown widely among the Aegean islands for the production of sweet white wines. Muscats are the wines that taste more like grape-juice than any other – but the high sugar levels ensure they are also among the most alcoholic of wines, too. Known as Moscato in Italy, the grape is much used for making sweet sparkling wines, as in Asti Spumante or Moscato d'Asti. There are several appellations in south-west France for inexpensive Muscats made rather like port, part-fermented before the addition of grape alcohol to halt the conversion of sugar into alcohol, creating a sweet and heady *vin doux naturel.* Dry Muscat wines, when well made, have a delicious sweet aroma but a refreshing light touch with flavours reminiscent variously of orange blossom, wood smoke and grapefruit.

must – New-pressed grape juice prior to fermentation.

Navarra – DO (Denominacion de Origen) wine-producing region of northern Spain adjacent to, and overshadowed by, Rioja. Navarra's wines can be startlingly akin to their neighbouring rivals, and sometimes rather better value for money.

négociant – In France, a dealer-producer who buys wines from growers and matures and/or blends them for sale under his or her own label. Purists can be a bit sniffy about these entrepreneurs, claiming that only the vine-grower with his or her own winemaking set-up can make truly authentic stuff, but the truth is that many of the best wines of France are négociant-produced – especially at the humbler end of the price scale. Négociants are often identified on wine labels as *négociant-éleveur* (literally 'dealer-bringer-up'), meaning that the wine has been matured, blended and bottled by the party in question.

Negro Amaro – Black grape variety mainly of Apulia, the fast-improving wine region of south-east Italy. Dense earthy red wines with ageing potential and plenty of alcohol. The grape behind Copertino.

Nero d'Avola – Black grape variety of Sicily and southern Italy. It makes deep-coloured wines which, given half a chance, can develop intensity and richness with age.

non-vintage – A wine is described as such when it has been blended from the harvests of more than one year. A non-vintage wine is not necessarily an inferior one, but under quality-control regulations around the world, still table wines most usually derive solely from one year's grape crop to qualify for appellation status. Champagnes and sparkling wines are mostly blended from several vintages, as are fortified wines such as basic port and sherry.

nose – In the vocabulary of the wine taster, the nose is the scent of a wine. Sounds a bit dotty, but makes a sensible-enough alternative to the rather bald 'smell'. The use of the word 'perfume' implies that the wine smells particularly good. 'Aroma' is used specifically to describe a wine that smells as it should, as in 'this Burgundy has the authentic strawberry-raspberry aroma of Pinot Noir' (see **Pinot Noir**).

nutskin – describing a red wine, this alludes to the sort of tongue-tingling dryness you get when biting through the papery, bitter skin of an almond.

Oltrepo Pavese – Wine-producing zone of Piedmont, north-west Italy. The name means 'south of Pavia across the [river] Po' and the wines, both white and red, can be excellent quality and value for money.

organic wine – As in other sectors of the food industry, demand for organically made wine is – or appears to be – growing. As a rule, a wine qualifies as organic if it comes entirely from grapes grown in vineyards cultivated without the use of synthetic materials, and made in a winery where chemical treatments or additives are shunned with similar vigour. In fact, there are plenty of winemakers in the world using organic methods, but who disdain to label their bottles as such. Wines that do brazenly proclaim their organic status tend to carry the same sort of premium as their counterparts round the corner in the fruit, vegetable and meat aisles. The upshot is that there is a very limited choice of organic wine at under a fiver. There is no single worldwide (or even Europe-wide) standard for organic food or wine, so you pretty much have to take the producer's word for it.

Pasqua – One of the biggest and, it should be said, best wine producers of the Veneto region of north-west Italy.

Passetoutgrains – Bourgogne Passetoutgrains is a generic appellation of the Burgundy region. The word loosely means 'any grapes allowed' and is supposed specifically to designate a red wine made with Gamay grapes as well as Burgundy's principal black variety, Pinot Noir, in a ratio of two parts Gamay to one of Pinot. The wine is usually relatively inexpensive, and relatively uninteresting too.

Periquita – Black grape variety of southern Portugal. Makes rather exotic spicy reds. The name means little parrot.

Petit Verdot – Black grape variety of Bordeaux used to give additional colour, density and spiciness to Cabernet Sauvignon-dominated blends. Strictly a minority player at home, but in Australia and California it is grown as the principal variety for some big hearty reds of real character.

Petite Sirah – Black grape variety of California and Latin America known for plenty of colour and long life. Not related to the Syrah of the Rhône.

petrol – When white wines from certain grapes, especially Riesling, are allowed to age in the bottle for longer than a year or two, they can take on a spirity aroma reminiscent of petrol or diesel. In grand mature German wines, this is considered a very good thing.

Picpoul de Pinet – Obscure white grape variety of the southern Rhône region of France occasionally makes interesting floral dry whites.

Piemonte – North-west province of Italy, known to us as Piedmont, known for the *spumante* (*q.v.*) wines of the town of Asti, plus expensive Barbaresco and Barolo and better-value varietal red wines from Barbera and Dolcetto grapes.

Pinot Blanc – White grape variety principally of Alsace, France. Florally perfumed, exotically fruity dry white wines.

Pinot Grigio – White grape variety of northern Italy. Wines bearing its name have become fashionable in recent times. Most are dull but the good wines have an interesting smoky-pungent aroma and keen, slaking fruit. Originally a French grape, known there as Pinot Gris, which is renowned for making lushly exotic – and expensive – white wines in the Alsace region.

Pinot Noir – The great black grape of Burgundy, France. It makes all the region's fabulously expensive red wines. Notoriously difficult to grow in warmer climates, it is nevertheless cultivated by countless intrepid winemakers in the New World intent on reproducing the magic appeal of red Burgundy. California and New Zealand have come closest, but rarely at prices much below those for the real thing. Some Chilean and Romanian Pinot Noirs are inexpensive and worth trying.

Pinotage – South Africa's own black grape variety. Makes red wines ranging from light and juicy to dark, strong and long-lived. It's a cross between Pinot Noir and a grape the South Africans used to call the Hermitage (thus the portmanteau name) but turned out to have been the Cinsault. Cheaper Pinotages tend to disappoint, but there has been an improvement in the standard of wines tasted during the year 2000.

Pouilly Fuissé – Village and AC of the Mâconnais region of southern Burgundy in France. Dry white wines from Chardonnay grapes. Wines are among the highest-rated of the Mâconnais.

Pouilly Fumé – Village and AC of the Loire Valley in France. Dry white wines from Sauvignon Blanc grapes. Similar 'pebbly', 'grassy' or even 'gooseberry' style to neighbouring AC Sancerre. The notion put about by some enthusiasts that Pouilly Fumé is 'smoky' is surely nothing more than word-association with the name.

Primitivo – Black grape variety of southern Italy, especially the region of Apulia/Puglia. The wines are typically dense and dark in colour with plenty of alcohol, and have an earthy, spicy style. Often a real bargain. It is closely related to California's Zinfandel, which makes purple, brambly wines of a very different hue.

Prosecco – White grape variety of Italy's Veneto region that gives its name to a light, sparkling and cheap wine much appreciated locally, but not widely exported.

Puglia – The region occupying the 'heel' of southern Italy, and one of the world's fastest-improving sources of inexpensive wines. Modern winemaking techniques and large regional grants from the EU are at least partly responsible.

QbA – On a German wine label stands for *Qualitätswein bestimmter Anbaugebiet.* It means 'quality wine from a designated area' and implies that the wine is made from grapes with a minimum level of ripeness, but it's by no means a guarantee of exciting quality. Only wines labelled QmP (see next entry) can be depended upon to be special.

QmP – On a German wine label it stands for *Qualitätswein mit Prädikat.* These are the serious wines of Germany, made without the addition of sugar to 'improve' them. To qualify for QmP status, the grapes must reach a level of ripeness as measured on a sweetness scale – all according to Germany's fiendishly complicated wine-quality regulations. Wines from grapes that reach the stated minimum level of sweetness qualify for the description of Kabinett. The next level up earns the rank of Spätlese, meaning 'late-picked'. Kabinett wines can be expected to be dry and brisk in style, and Spätlese wines a little bit riper and fuller. The next grade up, Auslese, meaning 'selected harvest', indicates a wine made from super-ripe grapes; it will be golden in colour and honeyed in flavour. A generation ago, these wines were as valued, and as expensive, as any of the world's grandest appellations, but the collapse in demand for German wines in the UK – brought about by the disrepute rightly earned for floods of filthy Liebfraumilch – means they are now seriously undervalued. Majestic has an unrivalled range of great bargains from Germany.

Quincy – AC of Loire Valley, France, known for pebbly-dry white wines from Sauvignon grapes. The wines are forever compared to those of nearby and much better-known Sancerre – and Quincy often represents better value for money. Pronounced 'KAN see'.

Quinta – Portuguese for farm or estate. It precedes the names of many of Portugal's best-known wines. It is pronounced 'KEEN ta'.

racy – Evocative wine-tasting description for wine that thrills the tastebuds with a rush of exciting sensations. Good Rieslings often qualify.

raisiny – Wines from grapes that have been very ripe or overripe at harvest can take on a smell and flavour akin to the concentrated, heat-dried sweetness of raisins. As a minor element in the character of a wine, this can add to the appeal but as a dominant characteristic it is a fault.

Reserva – In Portugal and Spain this has genuine significance. The Portuguese use it for special wines with a higher alcohol level and longer ageing, although the precise periods vary between regions. In Spain, especially in the Navarra and Rioja regions, it means the wine must have had at least a year in oak and two in bottle before release.

reserve – Applied to French (as *Réserve*) or other wines, this implies special-quality, longer-aged wines, but has no official significance.

Retsina – The universal white wine of Greece. It has been traditionally made in Attica, the region of Athens, for a very long time, and is said to owe its origins and name to the ancient custom of sealing amphorae (terracotta jars) of the wine with a gum made from pine resin. Some of the flavour of the resin inevitably transmitted itself into the wine, and the Ancient Greeks acquired a lasting taste for it.

Reuilly – AC of Loire Valley, France, for crisp dry whites from Sauvignon grapes. Pronounced 'RUH yee'.

Ribatejo – Emerging wine region of Portugal. Worth seeking out on labels of red wines, in particular, because new winemakers are producing lively stuff from distinctive indigenous grapes such as Castelao and Trincadeira.

Ribera del Duero – Classic wine region of north-west Spain lying along the river Duero (which crosses the border to become Portugal's Douro, forming the valley where port comes from). It is the home to an estate rather oddly named Vega Sicilia, where red wines of epic quality are made and sold at equally epic prices. Further down the scale, some very good reds are made too.

Riesling – The noble grape variety of Germany. It is correctly pronounced 'REEZ ling', not 'RICE ling'. Once notorious as the grape behind all those boring 'medium' Liebfraumilches and Niersteiners, this grape has had a bad press. In fact, there has never been much, if any, Riesling in Germany's cheap-and-nasty plonks. But the country's best wines, the so-called *Qualitätswein mit Prädikat* grades (see **QmP**), are made almost exclusively with Riesling. These wines range from crisply fresh and appley styles to extravagantly fruity, honeyed wines from late-harvested grapes. Excellent Riesling wines are also made in Alsace and now in Australia.

Rioja – The principal fine-wine region of Spain, in the country's north-east. The pricier wines are noted for their vanilla-pod richness from long ageing in oak casks. Younger wines, labelled variously *joven* (young) and *sincrianza* (meaning they are without barrel-ageing – see **crianza**), are cheaper and can make relishable drinking.

Ripasso – A particular style of Valpolicella wine. New wine is partially re-fermented in vats that have been used to make the 'recioto' reds of Valpolicella, and the effect is to create a bigger, smoother (and more alcoholic) version of usually light and pale Valpolicella.

Riserva – In Italy, a wine made only in the best vintages, and allowed longer ageing in cask and bottle.

Rivaner – Alternative name for Germany's Müller-Thurgau grape, the life-blood of Liebfraumilch.

Riverland – Vineyard region to the immediate north of the Barossa Valley of South Australia, extending east into New South Wales.

rosso – Red wine, Italian.

Rosso Conero – DOC red wine made in the environs of Ancona in the Marches, Italy. Made from the Montepulciano grape, the wine can provide excellent value for money.

Ruby Cabernet – Black grape variety of California, created by crossing Cabernet Sauvignon and Carignan. Makes soft and squelchy red wine at home and in South Africa.

Rueda – DO of north-west Spain making first-class refreshing dry whites from the indigenous Verdejo grape, imported Sauvignon grape, and others. Exciting quality – and prices, so far, are keen.

Rully – AC of Chalonnais region of southern Burgundy, France. Whites wines from Chardonnay and red wines from Pinot Noir grapes. Both can be very good and are substantially cheaper than their more northerly Burgundian neighbours. Pronounced 'ROO yee'.

Salento – Up and coming wine region of southern Italy. Many good bargain reds from local grapes including Nero D'Avola and Primitivo.

Sancerre – Appellation Contrôlée of the Loire Valley, France, renowned for flinty-fresh Sauvignon whites and rarer Pinot Noir reds. These wines are never cheap, and recent tastings make it plain that only the best-made, individual-producer wines are worth the money. Budget brands seem mostly dull.

Sangiovese – The local black grape of Tuscany, Italy. It is the principal variety used for Chianti and is now widely planted in Latin America – often making delicious, Chianti-like wines with characteristic cherryish-but-deeply-ripe fruit and a dry, clean finish. Chianti wines have become (unjustifiably) expensive in recent years and cheaper Italian wines such as those called Sangiovese di Toscana make a consoling substitute.

Santorini – Island of Greece's Cyclades was the site in about 1500BC of a tremendous volcanic explosion. The huge caldera of the volcano – a circular mini-archipelago – is now planted with vines producing very trendy and likeable dry white wines at fair prices.

Saumur – Town and appellation of Loire Valley, France. Characterful minerally red wines from Cabernet Franc grapes, and some whites.

Sauvignon Blanc – French white grape variety now grown worldwide. The wines are characterised by aromas of gooseberry, fresh-cut grass, even asparagus. Flavours are often described as grassy or nettley.

sec – Dry wine style, French.

secco – Dry wine style, Italian.

Semillon – White grape variety originally of Bordeaux, where it is blended with Sauvignon Blanc to make fresh dry whites and, when harvested very late in the season, the ambrosial sweet whites of Barsac, Sauternes and other appellations. Even in the driest wines, the grape can be recognised from its honeyed, sweet-pineapple, even banana-like aromas. Now widely planted in Australia and Latin America, and frequently blended with Chardonnay to make interesting dry whites.

sherry – The great aperitif wine of Spain, centred on the Andalusian city of Jerez (from which the name sherry is an English corruption). There is a lot of sherry-style wine in the world, but only the authentic wine from Jerez and the neighbouring producing towns of Puerta de Santa Maria and Sanlucar de Barrameida may label their wines as such. The Spanish drink real sherry – very dry and fresh, pale in colour and served well-chilled – called fino and manzanilla, and darker but naturally dry variations called amontillado, palo cortado and oloroso. The stuff sold under the big brand names for the British market are sweetened, coloured commercial yuck for putting in trifles or sideboard decanters to gather dust. The sherries recommended in this book are all real wines, made the way the Spanish like them.

Shiraz – Australian name for the Syrah grape. Aussie Shirazzes, unlike their silkily-spicy southern France counterparts, tend to be big, muscular and alcoholic wines with earthy darkness.

Sogrape – The leading wine company of Portugal, which built its fortune on Mateus Rosé. Sogrape is based in the Douro region, where port comes from, and makes many excellent table wines both locally and further afield. In 2002, Sogrape added the huge port (and sherry) house of Sandeman to its port-making interests.

Somontano – Wine region of north-east Spain. Name means 'under the mountains' – in this case the Pyrenees – and the region has had DO status only since 1984. Much innovative winemaking here, with 'New World' styles emerging. Some very good buys. A region to watch.

souple – French wine-tasting term translates to 'supple' or even 'docile' as in 'pliable' but I understand it in the vinous context to mean muscular but soft – a wine with tannin as well as soft fruit.

Spätlese – see QmP

spirity – Some wines, mostly from the New World, are made from grapes so ripe at harvest that their high alcohol content can be detected through a mildly burning sensation on the tongue, similar to the effect of sipping a spirit.

spritzy – Describes a wine with a barely detectable sparkle. Some young wines are intended to have this elusive fizziness; in others it is a fault.

spumante – Sparkling wine of Italy. Asti Spumante is the best known, from the town of Asti in the north-west Italian province of Piemonte (Piedmont). The term describes wines that are fully sparkling. *Frizzante* wines have a less-vigorous mousse.

stalky – A useful tasting term to describe red wines with flavours that make you think the stalks from the grape bunches must have been fermented along with the must (juice). Young Bordeaux reds very often have this mild astringency. In moderation it's fine, but if it dominates it probably signifies the wine is at best immature and at worst badly made.

Stellenbosch – Town and region at the heart of South Africa's burgeoning wine industry. It's an hour's drive from Capetown and the source of much of the country's cheaper wine. Quality is variable, and the name Stellenbosch on a label can't (yet, anyway) be taken as a guarantee of quality.

stony – Wine-tasting term for keenly dry white wines. It's meant to indicate a wine of purity and real quality, with just the right match of fruit and acidity.

structured – Good wines are not one-dimensional, they have layers of flavour and texture. A structured wine has phases of enjoyment: the 'attack' or first impression in the mouth; the middle palate as the wine is held in the mouth; the lingering aftertaste.

summer fruit – Wine-tasting term intended to convey a smell or taste of soft fruits such as strawberries and raspberries – without having to commit too specifically to which.

Superiore – On labels of Italian wines, this is more than an idle boast. Under DOC rules, wines must qualify for the Superiore designation by reaching one or more specified quality levels, usually a higher alcohol content or an additional period of maturation. Frascati, for example, qualifies for DOC status at 11.5 per cent alcohol, but to be classified Superiore it must have 12 per cent alcohol.

sur lie – 'On the lees'. It's a term now widely used on the labels of Muscadet wines, signifying that after fermentation has died down, the new wine has been left in the tank over the winter on the lees – the detritus of yeasts and other interesting compounds left over from the turbid fermentation process. The idea is that additional interest is imparted into the flavour of the wine.

Syrah – The noble grape of the Rhône Valley, France. Makes very dark, dense wine characterised by peppery, tarry aromas. Now planted all over southern France and farther afield. In Australia, where it makes wines ranging from disagreeably jam-like plonks to wonderfully rich and silky keeping wines, it is known as the Shiraz.

Tafelwein – Table wine, German. The humblest quality designation – doesn't usually bode very well.

tank method – Bulk-production process for sparkling wines. Base wine undergoes secondary fermentation in a large, sealed vat rather than in individual closed bottles. Also known as the Charmat method after the name of the inventor of the process.

tannin – Well-known as the film-forming, teeth-coating component in tea, tannin is a natural compound occurring in black grape skins and acts as a natural preservative in wine. Its noticeable presence in wine is regarded as a good thing. It gives young everyday reds their dryness, firmness of flavour and backbone. And it helps high-quality reds to retain their lively fruitiness for many years. A grand Bordeaux red when first made, for example, will have purply-sweet, rich fruit and mouth-puckering tannin, but after ten years or so this will have evolved into a delectably fruity mature wine in which the formerly parching effects of the tannin have receded almost completely, leaving the shade of 'residual tannin' that marks out a great wine approaching maturity.

tarry – On the whole, winemakers don't like critics to say their wines evoke the redolence of road repairs, but I can't help using this term to describe the agreeable sweet 'burnt' flavour that is often found at the centre of the fruit in wines from Argentina, Italy and Portugal in particular.

tears – see **legs**

Tempranillo – The great black grape of Spain. Along with Garnacha (Grenache in France) it makes all red Rioja and Navarra wines and, under many pseudonyms, is an important or exclusive contributor to the wines of many other regions of Spain. It is also widely cultivated in South America.

tinto – On Spanish and Portuguese labels indicates a deeply coloured red wine. *Clarete* denotes a paler hue.

Toro – Quality wine region east of Zamora, Spain.

Torrontes – White grape variety of Argentina. Makes soft, dry wines often with delicious grapey-spicy aroma, similar in style to the classic dry Muscat wines of Alsace, but at more accessible prices.

Touraine – Region encompassing a swathe of the Loire Valley, France. Non-AC wines may be labelled Sauvignon de Touraine etc.

Trebbiano – The workhorse white grape of Italy. A productive variety that is easy to cultivate, it seems to be included in just about every ordinary white wine of the entire nation – including Frascati, Orvieto and Soave. It is the same grape as France's Ugni Blanc.

Trincadeira Preta – Portuguese black grape variety native to the port-producing vineyards of the Douro Valley (where it goes under the name Tinta Amarella). In southern Portugal, it produces dark and sturdy table wines.

trocken – 'Dry' German wine. It's a recent trend among commercial-scale producers in the Rhine and Mosel to label their wines with this description in the hope of reassuring consumers that the contents do not resemble the dreaded sugar-water Liebfraumilch-type plonks of the bad old days. But the description does have a particular meaning under German wine law, namely that there is only a low level of unfermented sugar lingering in the wine (9 grams per litre, if you need to know), and this can leave the wine tasting rather austere.

Ugni Blanc – The most widely cultivated white grape variety of France and the mainstay of many a cheap dry white wine. To date it has been better known as the provider of base wine for distilling into Armagnac and Cognac, but lately the name has been appearing on wine labels. Technology seems to be improving the performance of the grape. The curious name is pronounced 'Oonyee', and is the same variety as Italy's ubiquitous Trebbiano.

Vacqueyras – Village of the southern Rhône valley of France in the region better known for its generic appellation, the Côtes du Rhône. Vacqueyras can date its winemaking history all the way back to 1414, but has only been producing under its own village AC since 1991. The wines, from Grenache and Syrah grapes, can be wonderfully silky and intense, spicy and long-lived.

Valdepeñas – An island of quality production amidst the ocean of mediocrity that is Spain's La Mancha region – where most of the grapes are grown for distilling into the head-banging brandies of Jerez. Valdepeñas reds are made from a grape they call the Cencibel – which turns out to be a very close relation of the Tempranillo grape that is the mainstay of the fine but expensive red wines of Rioja. Again, like Rioja, Valdepeñas wines are matured in oak casks to give them a vanilla-rich smoothness. Among bargain reds, Valdepeñas is a name to look out for.

Valpolicella – Red wine of Verona, Italy. Good examples have ripe, cherry fruit and a pleasingly dry finish. Unfortunately, there are many bad examples of Valpolicella. Shop with circumspection. Valpolicella Classico wines, from the best vineyards clustered around the town, are more reliable. Those additionally labelled superiore have higher alcohol and some bottle-age.

vanilla – Ageing wines in oak barrels (or, less picturesquely, adding oak chips to wine in huge concrete vats) imparts a range of characteristics including a smell of vanilla from ethyl vanilline naturally given off by oak.

varietal – A varietal wine is one named after the grape variety (one or more) from which it is made. Nearly all everyday wines worldwide are now labelled in this way. It is salutary to contemplate that just 20 years ago, wines described thus were virtually unknown outside Germany and one or two quirky regions of France and Italy.

vegan-friendly – My informal way of noting that a wine is claimed to have been made not only with animal-products-free finings (see **vegetarian wine**) but without any animal-related products whatsoever, such as manure in the vineyards.

vegetal – A tasting note definitely open to interpretation. It suggests a smell or flavour reminiscent less of fruit (apple, pineapple, strawberry and the like) than of something leafy or even root-based. Some wines are evocative (to some tastes) of beetroot, cabbage or even unlikelier vegetable flavours – and these characteristics may add materially to the attraction of the wine.

vegetarian wine – Given that proper wine consists of nothing other than grape juice and the occasional innocent natural additive, it might seem facile to qualify it as a vegetarian product. But most wines are 'fined' – clarified – with animal products. These include egg whites, isinglass from fish bladders and casein from milk. Gelatin, a beef by-product briefly banned by the UK government at the hysterical height of the BSE scare, is also used. Consumers who prefer to avoid contact, however remote, with these products, should look out for wines labelled suitable for vegetarians and/or vegans. The wines will have been fined with bentonite, an absorbent clay first found at Benton in the US state of Montana.

Verdelho – Portuguese grape variety once mainly used for a medium-dry style of Madeira, also called Verdelho, but now rare. The vine is now prospering in Australia, where it can make well-balanced dry whites with fleeting richness and lemon-lime acidity.

Verdicchio – White grape variety of Italy best known in the DOC zone of Castelli di Jesi in the Adriatic wine region of the Marches. Simple dry white wines once better known for appearing in naff amphora-style bottles.

Vermentino – White grape variety principally of Italy, especially Sardinia. Makes florally scented soft dry whites.

vin de liqueur – Sweet style of white wine mostly from the Pyrenean region of south-westernmost France, made by adding a little spirit to the new wine before it has fermented out, halting the fermentation and retaining sugar.

Vin Délimité de Qualité Supérieur – Usually abbreviated to VDQS, is a French wine-quality designation between Appellation Contrôlée and vin de pays. To qualify, the wine has to be from approved grape varieties grown in a defined zone. This designation is gradually disappearing.

vin de pays – 'Country wine' of France. The French map is divided up into more than a hundred vin de pays regions. Wine in bottles labelled as such must be from grapes grown in the nominated zone or *département*. Some vin de pays areas are huge: the Vin de Pays d'Oc (named after the Languedoc region) covers much of the Midi and Provence. Plenty of wines bearing this humble designation are of astoundingly high quality and certainly compete with 'New World' counterparts for interest and value.

Vin de Pays Catalan – Zone of sub-Pyrenees region (Roussillon) of south-west France.

Vin de Pays de l'Hérault – Zone within Languedoc-Roussillon region of south-west France.

Vin de Pays des Coteaux du Luberon – Zone of Provence, France.

Vin de Pays des Côtes de Gascogne – Zone of 'Gascony' region in south-west France.

Vin de Pays de Vaucluse – Zone of southern Rhône Valley, France.

Vin de Pays d'Oc – Largest of the zones, encompasses much of the huge region of the Languedoc of south-west France. Many excellent wines are sold under this classification, particularly those made in appellation areas from grapes not permitted locally.

Vin de Pays du Gers – Zone of south-west France including Gascony. White wines principally from Ugni Blanc and Colombard grapes.

Vin de Pays du Jardin de la France – Zone of the Loire Valley, France.

vin de table – The humblest official classification of French wine. Neither the region, grape varieties nor vintage need be stated on the label. The wine might not even be French. Don't expect too much from this kind of 'table wine'.

vin doux – Sweet, mildly fortified wine mostly of France, usually labelled *vin doux naturel*. A little spirit is added during the winemaking process, halting the fermentation by killing the yeast before it has consumed all the sugars – hence the pronounced sweetness of the wine.

vinho de mesa – 'Table wine' of Portugal.

vino da tavola – The humblest official classification of Italian wine. Much ordinary plonk bears this designation, but the bizarre quirks of Italy's wine laws dictate that some of that country's finest wines are also classed as mere *vino da tavola* (table wine). If an expensive Italian wine is labelled as such, it doesn't necessarily mean it will be a disappointment.

vino de mesa – 'Table wine' of Spain. Usually very ordinary.

vintage – The grape harvest. The year displayed on bottle labels is the year of the harvest. Wines bearing no date have been blended from the harvests of two or more years.

Viognier – A grape variety once exclusive to the northern Rhône Valley in France where it makes a very chi-chi wine, Condrieu, usually costing up to £20. Now, the Viognier is grown more widely, in North and South America as well as elsewhere in France, and occasionally produces soft, marrowy whites that echo the grand style of Condrieu itself.

Viura – White grape variety of Rioja, Spain. Also widely grown elsewhere in Spain under the name Macabeo (*q.v.*). Wines have a blossomy aroma and are dry, but sometimes soft at the expense of acidity.

Vouvray – AC of the Loire Valley, France, known for still and sparkling dry white wines and sweet, still whites from late-harvested grapes. The wines, all from Chenin Blanc grapes, have a unique capacity for unctuous softness combined with lively freshness – an effect best portrayed in the demi-sec (slightly sweet) wines, which can be delicious and keenly priced. Unfashionable, but worth looking out for.

weight – In an ideal world the weight of a wine is determined by the ripeness of the grapes from which it has been made. In some cases the weight is determined merely by the quantity of sugar added during the production process. A good, genuine wine described as having weight is one in which there is plenty of alcohol and 'extract' – colour and flavour from the grapes. Wine enthusiasts judge weight by swirling the wine in the glass and then examining the 'legs' or 'tears' left clinging to the inside of the glass after the contents have subsided. Alcohol gives these runlets a dense, glycerine-like condition, and if they cling for a long time, the wine is deemed to have weight – a very good thing in all honestly made wines.

Winzergenossenschaft – One of the many very lengthy and peculiar words regularly found on labels of German wines. This means a winemaking co-operative. Many excellent German wines are made by these associations of growers.

woodsap – A subjective tasting note. Some wines have a fleeting bitterness that is not a fault, but an interesting balancing factor amidst very ripe flavours. The effect somehow evokes woodsap.

Xarel-lo – One of the main grape varieties for cava, the sparkling wine of Spain.

Xinomavro – Black grape variety of Greece. It retains its acidity even in the very hot conditions that prevail in many Greek vineyards – where harvests tend to overripen and make cooked-tasting wines. Modern winemaking techniques are capable of making well-balanced wines from Xinomavro.

Yecla – Winemaking region of south-east Spain known for robust reds from Monastrell grapes.

yellow – White wines are not white at all, but various shades of yellow – or, more poetically, gold. Some white wines with opulent richness have a flavour I cannot resist calling yellow – reminiscent of butter.

Zefir – Hungarian white grape variety that can (on a good day) produce spicy dry wine rather like the Gewürztraminer of Alsace.

Zenit – Hungarian white grape variety. Dry wines.

Zinfandel – Black grape variety of California. Makes brambly reds, some of which can age very gracefully, and 'blush' whites – actually pink, because a little of the skin colour is allowed to leach into the must. The vine is also planted in Australia and South America. The Primitivo of southern Italy is said to be a related variety, but makes a very different kind of wine.

German wine names remain a mystery to most shoppers – this Tesco wine majors on the style Spätlese, signifying a late-picked, sweeter style

Wine rituals

There has always been a lot of nonsense talked about the correct ways to serve wine. Red wine, we are told, should be opened and allowed to 'breathe' before pouring: white wine should be chilled. Wine doesn't go with soup, tomatoes or chocolate. You know the sort of thing.

It would all be simply laughable except that these daft conventions do make so many potential wine lovers nervous about the simple ritual of opening a bottle and sharing it around. Here is a short and opinionated guide to the received wisdom.

Breathing

Simply uncorking a wine for an hour or two before you serve it will make absolutely no difference to the way it tastes. However, if you wish to warm up an icy bottle of red by placing it near (never on) a radiator or fire, do remove the cork first. As the wine warms, even very slightly, it gives off a gas that will spoil the flavour if it cannot escape.

Chambré-ing

One of the more florid terms in the wine vocabulary. The idea is that red wine should be at the same temperature as the room (*chambre*) you're going to drink it in. In fairness, it makes sense – although the term harks back to the days when the only people who drank wine were those who could afford to keep it in the freezing-cold vaulted cellars beneath their houses. The ridiculously high temperatures to which some homes are raised by central heating systems today are really far too warm for wine. But presumably those who live in such circumstances do so out of choice, and will prefer their wine to be similarly overheated.

Chilling

Drink your white wine as cold as you like. It's certainly true that good whites are at their best at a cool rather than at an icy temperature, but cheap and characterless wines can be improved immeasurably if they are cold enough – the anaesthetising effect of the temperature removes all sense of taste. Pay no attention to notions that red wine should not be served cool. There are plenty of lightweight reds that will respond very well to an hour in the fridge.

Corked wine

Wine trade surveys reveal that far too many bottles are in no fit state to be sold. The cork is very often cited as the villain. Cut from the bark of cork-oak trees cultivated for the purpose in Portugal and Spain, these natural stoppers have done sterling service for 200 years, but now face a crisis of confidence among wine producers. A diseased or damaged cork can make the wine taste stale because air has penetrated, or musty-mushroomy due to a chemical reaction. These faults in wine, known as corked or corky, should be immediately obvious, even in the humblest bottle, so you should return the bottle to the supplier and demand a refund. A warning here. Bad corks tend to come in batches. It might be wise not to accept another bottle of the same wine, but to choose something else.

Today, more and more wine producers are opting to close their bottles with polymer bungs. Some are designed to resemble the 'real thing' while others come in a rather disorienting range of colours – including black. There seems to be no evidence that these synthetic products do any harm to the wine, but it might not be sensible to 'lay down' bottles closed with polymer. The effects of years of contact with these materials are yet to be scientifically established. (*See also* Closures, pages 25–27.)

Corkscrews

The best kind of corkscrew is the 'waiter's friend' type. It looks like a pen-knife, unfolding a 'worm' (the helix or screw) and a lever device which, after the worm has been driven into the cork (try to centre it) rests on the lip of the bottle and enables you to withdraw the cork with minimal effort. These devices are cheaper and longer-lasting than any of the more elaborate types, and are equally effective at withdrawing the new polymer bungs – which can be hellishly difficult to unwind from Teflon-coated 'continuous' corkscrews like the Screwpull.

Decanting

There are two views on the merits of decanting wines. The prevailing one seems to be that it is pointless and even pretentious. The other is that it can make real improvements to the way a wine tastes and is definitely worth the trouble.

I subscribe firmly to the second – and don't care if it makes me seem pretentious, because I know it works. Pouring young red wine into a decanter, jug or any other receptacle can utterly transform it.

To quote a specific example, I conducted an untaxing experiment by opening two bottles of an excellent Sicilian red wine, Inycon Merlot 2000, when some friends were coming for supper. I left one bottle as it was and decanted the other. One hour later the four of us were trying a glass from each.

'Not the same wine,' said one. 'One tastes so much 'softer' than the other,' said another. This was just what I wanted to hear, because the effect of glugging a wine into another container is to aerate it, allowing at least some of the 'hardness' in the front-flavours (the first sensation on the tongue) of the wine to dissipate and the underlying flavours – in this case delicious black-cherry, minty ripeness – to come through.

Wine from the bottle that had merely been opened was notably masked by a toughness bordering on bitterness, disguising the lush fruit beneath. The fact that the bottle had 'breathed' for an hour was clearly nil – as you would expect after exposing only the equivalent of a square centimetre of wine at the top to the air.

Of course it's all too easy to drift into the dangerous realms of pretentiousness here, but there's nothing like a real experiment to keep minds concentrated on the facts. Scientists, not usually much exercised by the finer nuances of wine, will tell you that exposure to the air causes wine to 'oxidise' – take in oxygen molecules that will quite quickly initiate the process of turning wine into vinegar – and anyone who has tasted a morning-after glass of wine will no doubt vouch for this.

But the fact that wine does oxidise is a real clue to the reality of the effects of exposure to air. Shut inside its bottle, a young wine is very much a live substance, jumping with natural, but mysterious, compounds that can cause all sorts of strange taste sensations. But by exposing the wine to air these effects are markedly reduced.

In wines that have spent longer in the bottle, the influence of these factors diminishes in a process called 'reduction'. In red wines the hardness of tannin – the natural preservative imparted into wine from the grape skins – gradually reduces, just as a raw purple colour darkens to ruby and later to orangey-brown.

I believe there is less reason for decanting old wines than new, unless the old wine has thrown a deposit that needs carefully to be poured off it. And in some light-bodied wines, such as older Rioja, decanting is probably a bad idea because it can accelerate oxidation all too quickly.

Glasses

Does it make any difference whether you drink your wine from a hand-blown crystal glass or Old Mother Riley's hobnail boot? Do experiment! Conventional wisdom suggests that the ideal glass is clear, uncut, long-stemmed and with a tulip-shaped bowl large enough to hold a generous quantity when only half filled. The idea is that you can hold the glass by its stalk rather than by its bowl. This gives an uninterrupted view of the colour, and prevents you smearing the bowl with your sticky fingers. By filling the glass only halfway, you give the wine a chance to 'bloom', showing off its wonderful perfume. You can then intrude your nose into the air space within the glass, without getting it wet, to savour the bouquet. It's all harmless fun, really – and quite difficult to perform if the glass is an undersized Paris goblet filled, like a pub measure, to the brim.

Washing up

If your wine glasses are of any value to you, don't put them in the dishwasher. Over time, they'll craze from the heat of the water and they will not emerge in the glitteringly pristine condition suggested by the pictures on some detergent packets. For genuinely perfect glasses that will stay that way, wash them in hot soapy water, rinse with clean hot water and dry immediately with a glass cloth kept exclusively for this purpose. Sounds like fanaticism, but if you take your wine seriously you'll see there is sense in it.

Keeping it

How long can you keep an opened bottle of wine before it goes downhill? Not long. A recorked bottle with just a glassful out of it should stay fresh until the day after but, if there is a lot of air inside the bottle, the wine will oxidise, turning progressively stale and sour. 'Wine saving' devices that allow you to withdraw the air from the bottle via a punctured, self-sealing rubber stopper are variably effective, but don't expect these to keep a wine fresh for more than a couple of re-openings. A crafty method of keeping a half-finished bottle is to decant it, via a funnel, into a clean half bottle and recork.

Storing it

Supermarket labels always seem to advise that 'this wine should be consumed within one year of purchase'. I think this is a wheeze to persuade customers to drink it up quickly and come back for more. Many of the more robust red wines are likely to stay in good condition for much more than one year, and plenty will actually improve with age. On the other hand, it is a sensible axiom that inexpensive dry white wines are better the younger they are. If you do intend to store wines for longer than a few weeks, do pay heed to the conventional wisdom that bottles are best stored in low, stable temperatures, preferably in the dark. Bottles closed with conventional corks should be laid on their side lest the corks dry out for lack of contact with the wine.

Wine and food

Wine is made to be drunk with food, but some wines go better with particular dishes than others. It is no coincidence that Italian wines, characterised by soft, cherry fruit and a clean, mouthdrying finish, go so well with the sticky delights of pasta.

But it's personal taste rather than national associations that should determine the choice of wine with food. And if you prefer a black-hearted Argentinian Malbec to a brambly Italian Barbera with your bolognese, that's fine.

The conventions that have grown up around wine and food pairings do make some sense, just the same. I was thrilled to learn in the early days of my drinking career that sweet 'dessert' wines can go well with strong blue cheese. As I don't much like puddings, but love sweet wines, I was eager to test this match – and I'm here to tell you that it works very well indeed as the end-piece to a grand meal in which there is cheese as well as pud on offer.

Red wine and cheese are supposed to be a natural match, but I'm not so sure. Reds can taste awfully tinny with soft cheeses such as Brie and Camembert, and even worse with goats' cheese. A really extravagant, yellow Australian Chardonnay will make a better match. Hard cheeses such as Cheddar and the wonderful Old Amsterdam (top-of-the-market Gouda) are better with reds.

And then there's the delicate issue of fish. Red wine is supposed to be a no-no. This might well be true of grilled and wholly unadorned white fish such as sole or a delicate dish of prawns, scallops or crab. But what about oven-roasted monkfish or a substantial winter-season fish pie? An edgy red will do very well indeed, and provide much comfort for the many among us who simply prefer to drink red wine with food, and white wine on its own.

It is very often the method by which dishes are prepared, rather than their core ingredients, that determines which wine will work best. To be didactic, I would always choose Beaujolais or summer-fruit-style reds such as those from Pinot Noir grapes to go with a simple roast chicken. But if the bird is cooked as *coq au vin* with a hefty, winey sauce, I would plump for a much more assertive red.

Some sauces, it is alleged, will overwhelm all wines. Salsa and curry come to mind. I have carried out a number of experiments into this great issue of our time, in my capacity as consultant to a company that specialises in supplying wines to Asian restaurants. One discovery I have made is that forcefully fruity dry white wines with keen acidity can go very well indeed with even fairly incendiary dishes. Sauvignon Blanc with Madras? Give it a try!

I'm also convinced, however, that some red wines will stand up very well to a bit of heat. The marvellously robust Argentinian reds that get such frequent mentions in this book are good partners to Mexican chilli-hot recipes and salsa dishes. The dry, tannic edge to these wines provides a good counterpoint to the inflammatory spices in the food.

Some foods are supposedly impossible to match with wine. Eggs and chocolate, for instance, are often cited as prime offenders. Yet legendary cook Elizabeth David's best-selling autobiography was entitled *An Omelette and a Glass of Wine,* and the affiliation between chocolates and champagne is an unbreakable one. Taste is, after all, that most personally governed of all senses. If your choice is a boiled egg washed down with a glass of claret, who is to say otherwise?

Italian reds frequently have a dry finish that suits them particularly well to starchy pasta dishes – Co-op Chianti (£3.79) is a good example

Index